HOW TO BECOME RICH

HOW TO BECOME RICH

12 Lessons I Learnt from Vedic and Puranic Stories

DEVDUTT PATTANAIK

Illustrations by the author

Published by
Rupa Publications India Pvt. Ltd 2019
161-B/4, Gulmohar House,
Yusuf Sarai Community Centre,
New Delhi 110049

Sales centres:
Bengaluru Chennai
Hyderabad Kolkata Mumbai

Copyright © Devdutt Pattanaik 2019
Illustrations Copyright © Devdutt Pattanaik 2019

The views and opinions expressed in this book are the author's own and the facts are as reported by him which have been verified to the extent possible, and the publishers are not in any way liable for the same.

All rights reserved.

No part of this publication may be reproduced, transmitted, or stored in a retrieval system, in any form or by any means, electronic, mechanical, photocopying, recording or otherwise, without the prior permission of the publisher.

P-ISBN: 978-93-5333-689-9
E-ISBN: 978-93-5333-690-5

Seventh impression 2025

10 9 8 7

The moral right of the author has been asserted.

This edition is for sale in the Indian Subcontinent only.

Design and typeset in Sabon by Special Effects Graphics Design Co., Mumbai

Printed in India

This book is sold subject to the condition that it shall not, by way of trade or otherwise, be lent, resold, hired out, or otherwise circulated, without the publisher's prior consent, in any form of binding or cover other than that in which it is published.

*Dedicated to all those who want
Lakshmi to walk their way*

Contents

Introduction		1
1	**Is Wanting to Become Rich Normal?** Annapoorna on Hunger	7
2	**How Do We Earn Money?** Brahma on Exchange	13
3	**How Do We Lose Money?** Brihaspati on Complacency	27
4	**Who Pays Our Bills?** Agastya on Obligations	33
5	**How Do We Save Money?** Satyabhama on Saving	39
6	**Why Do We Grab Money?** Kubera on Extortion and Exploitation	45
7	**How Do We Manage Money?** Ganesha on Accounting and Planning	51
8	**Why Can We Never Avoid Taxes?** Shukra on Fairness	61
9	**How Do We Guard Wealth?** Hanuman on Insurance and Will	69
10	**How Do We Attract Money?** Vishnu on Repeat Orders and Referrals	75
11	**How Do We Share Money?** Varuna on Charity and Investment	81
12	**How Do We Grow Money?** Shakambari on Debt and Equity	91
Conclusion		103
Acknowledgements		108

Introduction
What the Vedas and Puranas Taught Me about Money and Commerce

In India, we worship Lakshmi, the goddess of wealth. She is referred to a lot in the Vedas and Puranas. The Vedas are over 3,000 years old, while the Puranas are nearly 2,000 years old—together, the Vedas and Puranas represent a key source of Hindu knowledge.

In the Vedas, Lakshmi is called Shri. In Vedic hymns, she is invoked for grain, gold, cows, horses,

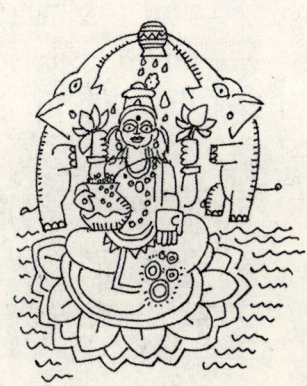

Lakshmi or Shri is the whimsical and restless goddess of wealth, affluence, abundance, auspiciousness and prosperity for Buddhists, Jains and Hindus.

children, fame and glory. In the Puranas, she is the elusive goddess—sought by Devas, Asuras, Yakshas and Rakshasas—who chooses Vishnu as her husband. Her arrival is considered good and auspicious (shubh, mangala) because when she comes we feel we are in paradise, or Swarga. Her departure is considered bad and inauspicious (ashubh, amangala), because when she leaves we slip into poverty, get trapped in debt, and feel like we are in hell, or Naraka, with no hope of escape.

In temples, the gods are bedecked with gold and jewels. In rituals, we use pots overflowing with food to represent abundance. During festivals, we clean our house and decorate the threshold with flowers, paint Lakshmi's footprints pointing indoors and light lamps at dusk so that she knows exactly where to come. Clearly, she is a much-desired goddess.

Yet, many relatives and friends, even gurus, tell us not to be 'money-minded', or that it is wrong to equate Lakshmi with money because Lakshmi is

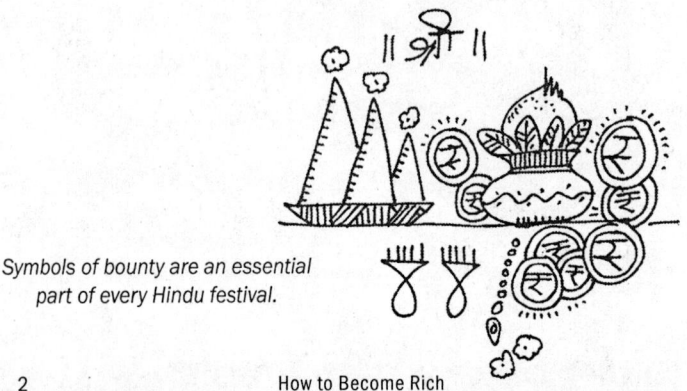

Symbols of bounty are an essential part of every Hindu festival.

spiritual while money is material. That if Lakshmi will come, then Saraswati, the goddess of learning, will go. The word 'commercial' is often used as an insult. Entrepreneurs, businessmen and traders are viewed with suspicion and considered thieves. Why?

Why this mockery of money (Lakshmi-ninda)? Why are we driving Lakshmi out of India instead of inviting her lovingly into our lives?

I realized that people were hiding something from Indian scriptures or overlooking some ideas, thereby ignoring them. This led me to relook at the stories of Lakshmi found in the Vedas and Puranas. Over time, I realized that Hinduism says a lot about economics (artha-shastra) at a personal level (sva-dharma), as well as at the social level (raj-dharma).

It dawned on me that we should look beyond literal meaning (shabda-artha) at metaphorical meaning (bhava-artha). When we say India was the land of the golden sparrow (sone ki chidiya), we don't mean India actually had birds whose wings were made of gold; we mean India, in ancient times, was very rich, exporting textiles and spices to places as far as Rome and importing gold.

Symbols are like pots and meaning is like water. If we look for meanings within the symbols of the Vedas and Puranas, we can learn many things about money and how to become rich:

- Lakshmi is considered a restless goddess (chanchal), which means wealth brings value only when it is circulated, not locked up. Those who grab and lock her up, get profit (labh) without happiness, not prosperity with happiness (shubh-labh).

- The concept of freedom (moksha) is related to repayment of debt (hrinn).

- Exchange (yagna), the fundamental concept of economics, is the cornerstone of dharma (governance).

- Charity that makes the receiver dependent (bhiksha) is frowned upon, whereas charity that makes the receiver independent (daan) is advocated.

- Wealth is to be seen as a fruit (phala), to be enjoyed now, and a seed (bija) to be invested for the future.

- Prithu was the first king of the earth who saw the earth as a cow (go-mata) and understood kingship as being the earth-cow's caretaker (go-pala). That is why the earth is called Prithvi. Giving away cows (go-daan) implies creating means of livelihood out of the earth. Consequently, the killing of cows (go-hatya) equals destroying the means of livelihood by destroying earth.

- Lakshmi (wealth) and Saraswati (knowledge) argue

The cow is a symbol of livelihood. To donate a cow is to create livelihood. To kill a cow is to destroy livelihood. The cow is a symbol of earth that we 'milk' for resources. Destroying the earth is akin to killing a cow.

until we discover Vidya-Lakshmi (knowledge of circulating wealth).

This book is the outcome of twenty years of research, and includes what I have learnt from writing and publishing over fifty books and more than a thousand columns on mythology.

The words 'mythology' and 'myth' upset people who follow the nineteenth-century British meaning of myth (worship of many gods) and religion (worship of one God). In the twenty-first century, mythology is the truth of a culture, the truth of a people, retold through stories, symbols and rituals. Mythology can speak of many gods (polytheism), one god (monotheism), as well as no god (atheism).

The Vedas and Puranas communicate the truth of Hindus through stories, symbols and rituals. It is neither fiction (nobody's truth) nor fact (everybody's truth). It is myth—somebody's truth. Different people have different truths. When we respect other people's truth, they respect our truth. When we do not respect other people's truth, nobody respects ours. In Hinduism, truth is not fixed or static. We are constantly moving from limited truth (mithya) to limitless truth (satya).

I have applied ideas related to Lakshmi in my own life and benefitted immensely. I have managed to earn a lot, enjoy a lot, save a lot, invest a lot and share a lot. I have learnt that being rich is about paying all bills, repaying all debts, and sharing wealth with others to make them independent and dependable.

These are my truths based on my reading of the Vedas and Puranas. I do not claim these are the only truths. My own truth expands when I re-read the Vedas and Puranas. May my expanding truth expand your truth. And always keep in mind:

Within infinite myths lies an eternal truth
Who sees it all?
Varuna has a thousand eyes
Indra, a hundred
You and I, only two.

1

Is Wanting to Become Rich Normal?
Annapoorna on Hunger

To become rich is to seek Lakshmi in our lives. Lakshmi is dhan (money), dhanya (food), sampatti (assets). Now, Hindus also worship Shiva who is known as the destroyer. Does Shiva destroy Lakshmi?

Not quite. Shiva destroys hunger—the craving for Lakshmi. How do we know this? Because we have heard the story of Shiva opening his third eye and destroying Kama.

Kama is popular as the god of sexual desires. But Kama is more than that. He is the god of hunger, all needs and wants, of all cravings, yearnings and ambitions. Kama makes us jealous of others who have what we want. He makes us determined to get what we want. He also makes us frustrated when we do not get what we want. When Kama strikes us with his arrows, we lose all restraint and want more and more and more. Hence, Kama is also known as Manmatha—he who twists our minds and drives us crazy.

After Kama was reduced to a heap of ash, Shiva smeared his body with that ash, went atop the mountain of stone known as Kailas and shut his eyes. He had no hunger, no desire, no dream, no greed, no ambition. He entered a state of tranquil meditation known as anand.

From the mountain, or parvat, on which Shiva sat came the goddess known as Parvati, also known as Uma and Gauri. She offered Shiva food and asked him to marry her. But Shiva did not eat the food. He refused to marry her. 'I have no hunger. So I want no food. I want no family. I am at peace.'

Parvati reminded him, 'You are the destroyer,' and disappeared. Shiva did not understand what she meant.

No hunger
I don't eat but I can be eaten

Need-based hunger
I eat and I can be eaten

Greed-based hunger
I only eat but I will not feed

Soon Shiva was surrounded by sounds of crying and wailing and whining. These grew louder and louder, and disturbed his peace. Shiva opened his eyes and found himself surrounded by Pisachas, or ghosts, spirits without bodies. Pisachas are also known as Shiva's followers, or Gana. 'Feed us. We are hungry,' they cried.

Shiva looked around and saw nothing alive in the world. With Kama gone, there was no hunger. Plants did not produce leaves to catch sunlight or roots to secure water. Deer stopped grazing. Tigers stopped hunting. Humans stopped farming and herding and weaving and trading and establishing villages and cities, making music and art. Without food, the plants withered and animals starved. Everything died eventually. Nothing was recreated or regenerated or reborn. Only the elements remained—the sky, wind, rocks and rivers. A world without life. A world full of wailing ghosts.

Shiva realized that without hunger there can be no life. Hunger creates craving for food. Food (anna) turns into flesh (anna-kosha). The body is hungry because flesh needs food to stay alive. The body has eyes to find food. The body has legs to reach food. The body has hands to catch food. The body has a mouth to consume food. The body has a mind that helps create food. After death the mind survives, retaining a memory of hunger, lingering as Pisachas, ghosts craving a food for flesh, and flesh for food.

Shiva realized why Parvati called him the destroyer. When he destroyed hunger, he had effectively destroyed the craving for Lakshmi, hence craving for life itself. To recreate life, to recreate the world, Lakshmi had to be sought, hunger was needed.

Shiva declared Parvati to be Mangala, the auspicious one, creator of family and home. He also called her Annapoorna, the goddess of food. He descended from the mountain and agreed to be her husband. In joy, Parvati set up a kitchen and around the kitchen emerged a city we now know as Kashi. The Pisachas were happy, as they finally had hope.

Life needs food. Food is the primary target of all organisms. From the word target, or Lakshmi, comes the idea of Lakshmi. Hunger is what makes us look for Lakshmi. Lakshmi is resources that help us stay alive and thrive. She is plant wealth, animal wealth, mineral wealth: food, cattle and gold. Today, we call her money. We chase Lakshmi in the way plants seek water, deer seek grass and tigers seek deer.

We need money to stay alive, for food, clothing and shelter, for comforts and luxuries. Without hunger, there will be no production, no servicing, no buying, no selling, no markets, no ambition, no innovation, no competition or collaboration, no growth. Hunger motivates us, drives us, propels us, goads us. If we are not hungry, we will not chase Lakshmi or find ways to make her walk our way. Hunger is what helps humans create culture and civilization. Hunger, uncontrolled, is what makes us jealous, aggressive and violent. It turns us into Pisachas, who are hungry all the time.

In India, those who cook their own food are considered poor. Those who can afford part-time cooks are considered middle class. Those who can afford a full-time cook are considered rich. Those who have to wash and iron their own clothes are considered poor. Those who can afford washing machines and can outsource ironing are considered middle class. Those who can afford a full-time housekeeper to wash and iron are considered rich. Kama motivates us to make the journey from poor to rich.

What are you hungry for?	Make notes to get clarity on your laksh, or goal
Your own house, car?	
Take care of your family?	
Success and admiration?	
Relax and pay others to do your work?	
Make more money than friends?	
Travel the world?	
Be free to shop for anything?	

Hunger can be classified as need and greed. We are told need is good and greed is bad. But how does one distinguish between ambition and greed? For the poor, the rich may appear greedy whereas the rich may see themselves as ambitious. Is a person who is content with his salary to be seen as someone who is not ambitious or someone who is not greedy? It is difficult to answer this question. Hence, we need to look at need and greed differently.

Need is seeking to satisfy our hunger and the hunger of those who feed us. Greed is being consumed by our own hunger at the cost of those who feed us. When we're in need, we seek Swarga for ourselves and others. In greed, we seek Swarga for ourselves even if it means pushing others into Naraka. If you are only interested in your own comfort and not that of your family, friends, employees, partners, vendors and society at large, then you are greedy.

Without hunger, we would not value Lakshmi. The more Lakshmi we have, the more comfortable our life can be. Need-based hunger creates delight, with the rich working to help the poor satisfy their hunger. Greed-based hunger creates quarrels, with the rich withholding food, forcing the hungry to attack them constantly.

Annapoorna's lesson
Wanting to become rich means wanting to enjoy and share a comfortable life. And that is perfectly normal.

2

How Do We Earn Money?
Brahma on Exchange

Brahma is called the creator of the Hindu world—from him emerged all living creatures. This means Brahma created hunger, hence life. Maybe that is why Hindus do not worship him, just like they do not worship Kama. There are stories of Shiva cutting the fifth head of Brahma to restrain his insatiable hunger.

Once, Brahma called all his children for a meal. When the food was served, he said they could eat but they could not bend their elbows! Now how can you eat when you cannot bend your elbow? Brahma said nothing.

Some children bent their head and licked the food. They became animals or Pashu. Some children complained and got angry. They became Asura. Some children disobeyed Brahma, grabbed the food and ran away. They became Rakshasa. Some Rakshasas hoarded food and refused to share. They became Yaksha.

The rest picked up the food and fed the person next to them, hoping someone would feed them in return. The one who fed the other, in the hope of getting fed, came to be known as Yajaman. The one who was fed, and had the option of returning the favour, became Devata. Yajaman was sensitive to Devata's hunger. He hoped the Devata would reciprocate and be sensitive to his own hunger.

Those who kept demanding and receiving food but not feeding others became Pisacha. Those who danced and sang in the hope of getting fed became Gandharva.

This was the origin of the Vedic ritual of yagna. Brahma established the yagna to make humans civilized. Plants grab Lakshmi (sunlight, water,

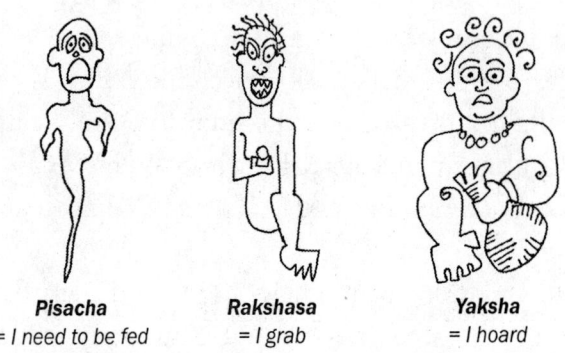

Pisacha
= I need to be fed

Rakshasa
= I grab

Yaksha
= I hoard

nutrients) to satisfy their hunger. Animals also grab Lakshmi (plants, animals) to satisfy their hunger. When humans grab, we are being Rakshasa.

What is your source of income?	What goods or services do you offer in exchange?	What is guaranteed tomorrow?
Allowance from parents		
Salary from job		
Grant from sponsor, patron or government		
Savings in bank		
Returns from business		

In a civilized society, humans do not need to grab—they get food from other humans, and they are expected to return the favour. This is exchange or yagna. To exchange, to feed others and be fed by others is dharma. Participating in yagna is dharma.

Asura
= I reclaim

Deva
= I repay

Gandharva
= I earn

What is the most common thinking pattern that you observe in yourself?	In crisis	In success
I must focus on what I want.		
I must think of others too.		
I must save for future.		
I owe the world.		
People can be trusted.		
Rich people are cheats.		

We earn by participating in yagna. The steps of yagna are simple: the Yajaman calls the Devata and gives the Devata something, expecting something in return. When the Yajaman gives, he says 'Svaha'—which means, 'that which is mine is now yours'. This makes Svaha an investment. Yajaman hopes that the Devata will reply with 'Tathastu'—which means, 'what you want you will get'. This makes Tathastu the return on investment (ROI). As Yajamans, we invest to get returns from others. This is full of risks, as the debt may not be repaid. As Devatas, others invest in us to get returns. This is high pressure, as the debt has to be repaid.

Now how does the Devata know what the Yajaman wants? The Yajaman expresses his wishes clearly before the yagna by doing Sankalpa and after the yagna by doing Phalastuti. Sankalpa means 'here is why I am going to perform the yagna'. Phalastuti is a reminder and means 'this is the fruit I expect for performing

this yagna'. Sankalpa is before giving and Phalastuti is after giving.

Only after Sankalpa does the Yajaman do avahan, or 'summoning the Devata'. If the Devata cannot fulfil his wish, he does not come. If the Devata is not satisfied with the Svaha, or offering, he does not satisfy the wishes of the Yajaman. If the Yajaman feels the Devata is not giving him what he wants, he does visarjan of the Devata, i.e. 'bids him farewell', and never calls him again. Instead he does avahan of another Devata.

We are all potential Yajamans. We can feed others in the hope of getting fed in the future. We can invest, and take the risk of not receiving anything in exchange. We are also potential Devatas. We grow up being fed by others: parents, family, friends, employers, employees, investors, investees, government, nature. If we keep eating and not feeding others, we behave like the Pisacha. We can repay our debt to family and society and nature. To remind us we are the Yajaman and the Devata, with the potential to feed one another, either to invest or repay debt, Hindus do namaste to each other.

Yagna means to give what you have to get what you want. This is the basic principle of economics, or artha-shastra. Brahma taught the value of exchange to Brihaspati and Shukra, who composed the earliest books on economics. Brahma also taught the value of exchange to Manu, who composed the dharma-shastra, as it is also the fundamental principle of humanity.

As long as we grab food, as long as we don't feed the other and repay the debt of being fed, we remain Rakshasa, Yaksha and Pisacha; in other words, uncivilized. To become human, we have to follow dharma. We have to feed those who feed us. We also can feed those who don't feed us. Yajaman gives and then hopes to get. Devata gets and then may give.

Civilized society is based on exchange. I feed someone and someone feeds me. Food can be goods, services or money.

List all your Devatas: those who owe you, and have to repay you (note: not just money)	List all your Yajamans: those who you have borrowed from, and have to repay (note: not just money)

Some people say yagna is a 'sacrifice' but in a sacrifice, you give but do not get. So yagna cannot be a sacrifice. Others say yagna is a 'contract' but in a contract, you are obliged to give and get. Yagna cannot be a contract because it is voluntary. Ideas like sacrifice and contract come to us from Judaism, Christianity and Islam—worldviews in which God created the world, made the rules, and expects humans—who accept the contract—to follow them. Those who follow the rules go to heaven, those who don't, go to hell. To follow the rules is to love God; to break them is to be tempted by the Devil. Most modern businesses and governments in India and abroad use this 'contract' model to earn and distribute money.

Yagna, by contrast, is completely voluntary. It is about taking risks. It is more about developing self-confidence than trying to control others. Hence there are no fixed rules. In the Vedas, 'God' is the potential within us to feed others. We can feed the hungry as Yajamans. We can feed those who feed us as Devatas. The more we give, the more divine we become.

Modern markets are based on contracts. This means the Devata is bound by law to repay what he owes the Yajaman. If the Yajaman is a seller, and gives goods and services, then he must get paid. If the Yajaman is a buyer, and gives money, then he must receive goods and services.

In a market, yagna is constantly taking place. We can be either Yajaman: who goes looking for customer-Devata, and offers them goods and services first, and then receives money later. Or we can be Devata: who accepts money from buyer-Yajamans first and then provides them with goods and services later. When we begin our careers, we are Yajaman, we seek Devatas who give us money. When we become successful, we become Devatas, chased by Yajaman offering us money for our goods and services.

As Yajaman or Devata, what is the food we give? Only two things: goods and services. What is the food we want? Money.

Goods can mean anything that people want, such as a broom. Services mean activities that people require, such as sweeping. You can sell brooms as goods, or sell sweeping as a service.

Goods include food, clothing, shelter, water, medicines, electricity, furniture, Internet, computers, books and information. Services include cooking, styling, engineering, healing, advising, consulting, teaching, governing, policing and housekeeping.

In the Vedas, those who make you think of other people's hunger are known as the Brahmins, because they help you expand (brah-) your mind (manas) and make you look (darshan) beyond your own hunger. When this happens, we want to become less like animals who grab food and more like humans who borrow, lend and exchange. This is a prerequisite for doing yagna properly. The Yajaman needs to be sensitive about the hunger of the Devata and the Devata has to be sensitive about the hunger of the Yajaman.

List all the goods you can offer as Svaha to your family, friends, company, society	List all the services i.e. skills you can offer as Svaha to family, friends, company, society

In the forest, or aranya, animals grab food. So do humans, unless we embrace the civilized way of yagna, or exchange. The place where people exchange goods and services is called a kshetra, or market, the cornerstone of civilized human settlement. He who establishes a kshetra is the Kshatriya. He ensures that exchange is respected, that people are not exploited, that what is given is not more than what is received, and what is received is not more than what is given. To ensure this is dharma.

Vaishyas or Vaniks are product creators and distributors. Shudras are service providers.

This is not a jati, or caste. Caste means a vocation that you inherit at birth. It is an old Indian economic system that is no longer viable or valid. This is varna, described in Vedas, as four psychological states that establishes civilized society.

Many people argue that Shudras are servants,

and so inferior and Brahmins are priests and, so, superior. They identify Brahmins as those who provide 'superior' services, for instance, taking care of temples, conducting weddings, teaching, and working as bureaucrats or accountants. For them, Kshatriyas are people who provide 'superior' services such as fighting wars, fighting law-breakers, fighting elections and fighting for reform and justice. They do not recognize Vaishyas as providers of trading services such as manufacturing, logistics, warehousing and banking. For them, Shudras are those in 'inferior' services such as sweeping the floor, plumbing and sanitation, construction, cooking food, working in factories and driving cars. Such thinking indicates ignorance (avidya) and ego (aham). Such people promote hierarchy based on 'purity' and disrespect labour.

From Lakshmi's point of view, there is no superior or inferior service. Different services just have different costs. Services earn us Lakshmi. Everyone who does service is a Shudra. Everyone who sells a product is a Vanik. In modern times, even goods-sellers are becoming service providers. The gap between goods and services is narrowing. We expect shopkeepers selling anything from books to gold, to provide quality customer service too.

Many IT companies provide services—such as call centres, business process outsourcing, knowledge process outsourcing. Politicians are doing public service by creating policies that benefit society. Bureaucrats are doing service by implementing policies. Gurus are also providing services by teaching yoga and providing emotional support. Soldiers are serving by defending their country. They are all Shudras, service providers. If you hesitate to use this word, or see this word as downmarket, remember you are suffering from ignorance (avidya) and ego (aham), also known as low spiritual index.

Those with a low spiritual index do not mind calling themselves servants (dasa) of god but treat their own servants, or rather service providers, disrespectfully. There are people who hold the 'seva' of a guru and of god in high regard but insult those who clean toilets and sewage drains, disrespectfully saying, 'We will not touch you'. They value medical services over housekeeping services.

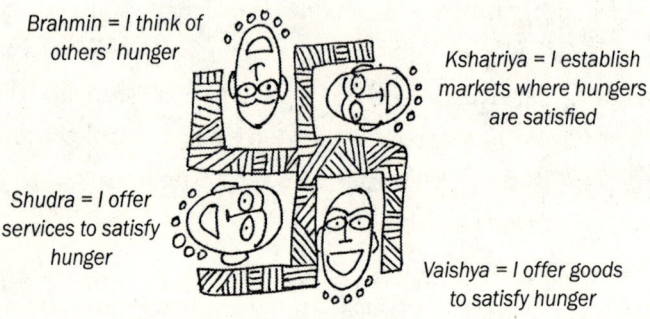

Brahmin = I think of others' hunger

Kshatriya = I establish markets where hungers are satisfied

Shudra = I offer services to satisfy hunger

Vaishya = I offer goods to satisfy hunger

Your psychological state (varna)	Give percentage...the four fields should add up to hundred
You believe in helping others to help yourself	
You create events and enterprises and opportunities where people can help each other	
You help yourself by offering things to others	
You help yourself by offering skills to others	

Those with a high spiritual index never say this job or this product is superior to that job or that product. They realize that every product, every job, every good, every service is bhog—that which is consumed by the hungry. Different Devatas need different bhogs. And different Yajamans have different bhogs to offer.

In a feudal agrarian society, the landowners control Lakshmi and give it to others at their discretion. Here, the goods-seller and service-provider are at the mercy of the landowners who identify themselves as gods, who expect submission and loyalty from devotees. This is not yagna. This is not the way of Rishis.

In dharma, exchange is key—exchange between equals. The Yajaman needs the Devata and the Devata needs the Yajaman. They acknowledge each other's hunger and nourish each other. Hence, they venerate each other by doing namaste. The Hindu greeting of joining palms is an acknowledgement of the divine within us that can feed the other, while being fed by others.

In dharma, we do namaste, to acknowledge the Devata within us who can become Yajaman. In adharma, the same gesture of namaste is reduced to an act of saluting, pleading and submitting by the meek to establish the dominance of the mighty. In dharma, Lakshmi moves freely from one side to another. In adharma, Lakshmi is held captive by one and distributed sparingly, giving rise to Alakshmi, the goddess of discontent and quarrels.

Brahma's lesson
To earn money, we must be sensitive to the hunger of customers and provide them with goods and services they want, so they give us our due as part of yagna, or exchange. If we do not think of customer needs and demands, we cannot do yagna.

3

How Do We Lose Money?
Brihaspati on Complacency

In the Vedas, there are a thousand hymns, most dedicated to inviting Indra to come to the yagna and receive his favourite food, Soma. In other words, the most popular Devata of the Vedic yagna was Indra.

Why did people invoke Indra? Because he had everything. His abode, Swarga, is paradise, full of treasures, trophies and fun. His wife, Sachi, is considered a form of Lakshmi.

Why did Indra have everything? Because he was constantly being called and offered Soma for making the Yajaman happy. Until he did not.

Indra lived a luxurious life—enjoying the dance of the Apsaras, the song of the Gandharvas, the intoxication of Varuni and the abundance of the Nandankana gardens. Life was like an endless party. Then one day, his throne began to shake. He feared he was about to fall from Swarga. He decided to investigate the matter.

He found a king called Sagar performing yagnas, offering Svaha to Devatas, but seeking nothing in exchange. Indra realized that Sagar's generosity was making him popular with the Devatas. He feared the Devatas would eventually declare Sagar to be their leader, their 'Indra', and they would forget the old Indra. Indra realized he was replaceable. He became insecure and jealous and angry. So he stole Sagar's horse and ensured Sagar could not make any more offerings to any Devata. Indra's throne stabilized. But only for some time.

Indra's throne wobbled once again. This time Indra saw a sage called Vishwamitra, seated still, eyes shut, performing tapasya to open his third eye and destroy Kama. If he succeeded, he would conquer hunger and would have no motivation to perform yagna. He would need no Lakshmi. So he would not need to call Indra and offer him Soma. Once again

Will people prefer buying from him instead of me?

he became insecure and frightened. He sent his most skilled Apsara, Menaka, to enchant Vishwamitra—to tell him about the wonders of Swarga: dance, music, intoxicants, unlimited fun. Menaka succeeded in tempting Vishwamitra. Indra was happy.

By disrupting Sagar's yagna, Indra ensured he could not be replaced. By tempting Vishwamitra, Indra ensured he was always in demand. He felt he was safe. The Yajaman would always seek him. And he would be the only one they could get. In other words, he had monopoly over the yagna. This made Indra feel secure and confident. Overconfident even.

The wealth on earth depended on the rains. When it rained, the wells were filled, the farms yielded rich harvests and the cattle had enough to eat. Regular rain meant prosperity, abundance, affluence. With rain, came Lakshmi. Now, as long as Yajamans performed yagna regularly, it rained regularly. But over time, the rains became erratic. Sometimes there was less rain, which caused drought. Sometimes the rain was excessive, causing flood. Indra, the rain-god, stopped being reliable. He was too busy enjoying his life in

Does he not want what I wish to sell?

Swarga, confident that people had no choice but to invoke him through yagna.

Indra was having so much fun that people started to complain. But Indra did not care. He even ignored Rishi Brihaspati, his advisor and coach on economic matters. Furious, Brihaspati cursed Indra that he would eventually be overshadowed by another god. According to the Vedas, this was Vishnu, Indra's younger brother.

We are all Indra as long as we have an income, as long as money keeps coming into our lives. It means we are offering either goods or services to satisfy the hunger of customers. We have income as long as people do not go elsewhere for goods and services. We have income as long as people want our goods and services. But there is always a Sagar or a Vishwamitra who can threaten our income.

Sagar is that product or service which can replace ours. Sagar is that new talent who can replace us. Sagar is the new technology that can replace what we have. Vishwamitra is that customer who does not want our services, who we have to entice using marketing, using

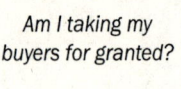
Am I taking my buyers for granted?

deals and discounts. The fear of competition and a lack of demand makes our thrones wobble constantly like Indra's. We are, therefore, always insecure. We lose money when our goods and services are replaced, or when there is no demand for our goods and services. Indra matters as long as he provides rain regularly. We matter only as long as we are relevant.

And when we have no competition, and we are always in demand, we risk becoming complacent, arrogant, demanding more and giving less, angering those who believe in exchange, who then seek out a new Devata. This is why monopoly eventually fails. Competition keeps us on our toes. Forces us to stay alert and innovate. Fear of declining demand keeps us on our toes, forces us to do better marketing and keep augmenting our skill set.

List the potential competition to your income (potential Sagar)	List customers on whom you depend for income (potential Vishwamitra)	List instances when you have taken your source of income for granted

Remember, you do not lose money by spending. That only creates debts—expenses that are booked, which you have to repay whether you earn or not. You lose money by not earning enough. And you do not earn enough when there are other people giving the same or better goods and services as you are, or if there is not enough demand for the goods and service you offer, or if you annoy customers so much that they do not want goods and services from you, and choose other Devatas to satisfy their hunger.

List how you are upgrading your goods and skills	List how you keep old customers happy	List how you find new customers

Brihaspati's lesson

We lose money when there is someone who can give better goods and services to the market than us, when there is no demand for the goods and services we offer, or if we become too lazy to take feedback from the market and improve.

4

Who Pays Our Bills?
Agastya on Obligations

Agastya, inspired by Shiva, shut his eyes and meditated, determined to open his third eye and destroy Kama. He did not want to be hungry. He did not want to be miserable. He wanted peace of mind.

But then he saw a vision: he saw his ancestors, or Pitrs, hanging upside down over a bottomless pit. They were crying. 'We gave you birth. We raised you, fed you, sheltered you, educated you. You owe us your life, and your body, and your knowledge. You are in our debt. You must repay us. You must help us be reborn. Otherwise, you will never be free. When you die, you too will be trapped in the land of the dead, like the Pisachas, forever hungry for a body, forever hungry for food. Create a child. Or at least adopt a child. Raise the next generation and repay your debt to the past generation.'

Agastya decided he would adopt children, raise them, repay his debt to his ancestors and return to his main goal of destroying Kama. He went around asking people if they could give him orphans he could adopt and take care of. People said, 'You have no house, no income. You live alone and have no property. Why would we let you take care of orphans? How will you feed them?'

So Agastya decided to produce his own children. For that he needed a wife. He went to a king and asked for the hand of the king's daughter in marriage. 'Sure, I will ask my daughter to marry you. But how will you repay the debt you owe me for giving you my daughter?'

The princess in question was called Lopamudra. She told Agastya, 'I will marry you and I will bear your children and take care of them. I will help you repay your debt to your ancestors. But I am a princess. I will want you to treat me like a princess and give me all the comforts my father gave me. You owe that to me if I am going to help you repay your debt to your ancestors.'

Agastya needed an income to repay his debt to Lopamudra and her father. He heard that Rakshasa Atapi had a lot of gold.

'I will give you gold if you eat the food I serve you,' said Atapi. Agastya was more than happy to do that to get the gold. The food turned out to be meat. Agastya, who preferred plant food, ate the meat as he had no choice. It was the only way to get the income he needed.

After Agastya had eaten, Atapi shouted, 'Vatapi, come out.' Agastya burped in satisfaction. Atapi was shocked. His brother, Vatapi, was a shape-shifter. Vatapi had turned into a goat that was killed to make the food for Agastya. When Atapi shouted, 'Vatapi, come out,' Vatapi was supposed to tear through Agastya's stomach and emerge. The two Rakshasa brothers would eat him with relish and keep all his possessions. That is how they had killed many travellers and had collected all their gold. Unfortunately for Atapi, Agastya had digested Vatapi before he could be summoned.

We need money to pay all that we owe the past. Our expenses are booked even before we start earning.

We carry the burden of debts, bills and responsibilities. To be debt-free is to attain moksha.

Atapi started to cry. 'Now what will I eat? You are not dead. I have nothing to eat. My brother is not alive. And I have no means of finding food in the future. All because of you Agastya. You are in my debt.'

'I did what you told me to do,' said Agastya. 'I ate your food. Now give me the gold. Just as I found a source of income, you have to find another source of income.' Atapi had no choice but to keep his end of the bargain.

Agastya gave half of Atapi's gold to Lopamudra's father. With the rest, he built a beautiful house for Lopamudra, complete with a pond full of fish, an orchard of fruit-bearing trees and a shed of cows that gave milk for food and dung for fuel. There they lived as husband and wife, had children and raised them.

When they were old, their youngest child said, 'You gave me life and raised me. I owe you. So I will fulfil your desire to meet Shiva and Shakti in Kashi.' Agastya was happy to hear this, but he and his wife had aged—he had no strength to walk and Lopamudra was blind. So the boy created a shoulder sling. On both sides of which were baskets. In one basket he carried Agastya and in the other he carried Lopamudra. Like this, he shouldered the weight of his parents and took them to Kashi.

In Kashi, Agastya found Shiva in the form of Bhairav serving as kotwal, the chief of police. Bhairav explained, 'Annapoorna helped give Pisachas a body as well as food for that body. In exchange, I protect her city. Likewise, your son is in your debt, and you are in Lopamudra's debt. There is no escape from debt. In life, you pay old debts and you incur new ones. Freedom, or moksha, comes only when you have repaid all your debts.'

Hrinn, or debt, is a central concept in Hinduism. All Hindus are expected to repay their debts five times over. First, to their ancestors, by raising the next generation of children. Second, to the divine within, by taking care of the body in which it resides. Third, to the divine without, by taking care of their community, even strangers. Fourth, to the ones who feed us, by providing them goods and services. Fifth, to nature, by taking care of plants and animals, rivers and mountains.

All living creatures—from plants to animals and humans, even kings and gods—are in debt. To be alive, is to be in debt of the world around us. We have to repay the parents who raise us, the family that protects us, our friends who support us, our communities that guide us, the world at large, which creates opportunities and keeps away threats, and finally nature itself, which sustains all cultures and civilizations. Practically speaking, we need to pay our bills or else we will always be in a debt trap. So we need Lakshmi.

Select obligations that you cannot shun	Prioritize (1 to 6)
To self	
To family	
To community	
To society	
To nature	

Many people who have to work to pay their bills, feel that those who inherit wealth from family are lucky. But such luck comes at a price. Those who get money from family are bound to obey their family to repay their debt: so they are forced to marry people they do not love, and be friends with people they do not like, and come to functions they hate. Despite all the money, they feel trapped. They cannot escape. It is the price of inherited wealth. Even the rich are in debt when they don't pay their own bills.

Agastya's lesson
We have to pay our own bills. Most of our bills are incurred even before we start earning. When other people pay our bills, we are in their debt. Sooner or later, the money lender will demand return one way or another.

5

How Do We Save Money?
Satyabhama on Saving

Once Indra asked Krishna for help, saying, 'Please defeat the Asura Naraka and bring back the treasures he has stolen.' Without a moment's thought, Krishna went to war, defeated the Asura and returned all of Indra's treasures. Satyabhama then asked Krishna, 'So what did Indra give you in exchange?'

'Nothing,' replied Krishna.

'Why? Is he not in your debt?'

'But I want nothing,' said Krishna with a smile.

'That's wonderful. But what about me? I want something. I want the Parijata tree from Indra's garden. Can you get that for me?' said Satyabhama.

Krishna asked Indra for this favour but he refused.

'This Parijata tree belongs in Swarga. I cannot let you take it to Dwarka.' Krishna was shocked by Indra's ingratitude. He realized Indra was exploiting him: when there is no exchange, there is exploitation. Furious, he fought Indra and forcibly took Parijata from Swarga and planted it in Dwarka for Satyabhama.

After the Parijata incident, Krishna vowed to first receive, only then give.

So when Krishna's friend Sudama came to visit Krishna, Krishna welcomed him home with the words, 'I am so happy to see you. Surely you have not come to meet me after so many years, empty-handed? Surely you have brought me a gift?' Very reluctantly, Sudama shared a small portion of puffed rice that he had managed to keep aside by not eating for three days. Krishna was delighted to receive this gift and began eating it with relish. Sudama was happy seeing his rich friend accept his poor gift. Krishna ate one fistful. Then another. He was about to finish it all when Satyabhama caught his hand and said, 'My husband. Will you not spare something for your family? Surely we need something too.'

Satyabhama knew if Sudama had asked for money directly, she would not have let Krishna pay. So Krishna had deliberately placed himself in debt by asking a gift from Sudama first. Now Krishna was obliged to repay. Satyabhama, as the good wife, had to support him.

Since Sudama had given Krishna all he had, Krishna was obliged to give Sudama all he had. But if he did that, how would Krishna's household survive? That is why Satyabhama asked Krishna to feed her too, reminding him of his family's hunger.

List all the Indras who have taken your help but not returned the favour even when they could	List all the Sudamas who have asked for help but you know can never help you in return

Later, when Sudama had left, Satyabhama told Krishna, 'Harischandra gave away all his wealth. After that, to help Vishwamitra, he had to earn money by selling himself, his wife and child as slaves. Do you want to sell us too when we have no money and you have to help more people like Sudama?'

'Don't worry,' said Krishna. 'I will always take care of the earth and the earth will feed us, in exchange. The earth is Go-mata, and I am her Go-pala. I protect her, and she nourishes me with her milk. I have been doing this since my days as a cowherd in Go-kula.'

Then Satyabhama asked, 'What did you eat on days when the cow did not give milk?'

Pat came Krishna's reply, 'Curds and butter and sweets

of cheese and ghee.' As he said this, he remembered how his mother, Yashoda, would shout at him if he drank up all the milk. She would give him only a third to consume. A third she would turn into cheese to be eaten in the weeks thereafter. The final third she would curdle to eat the day after. One half of the curd she would churn to make butter and buttermilk to consume on the following day. Half the butter would be turned into ghee, which could be used for months afterwards. By turning cow's milk into curd, butter, cheese and ghee, Yashoda made sure there was food for the days when the cows did not give milk.

Yashoda would tell Krishna to study the cows carefully. 'Look how she eats grass quickly and chews it at leisure. She stores food in one stomach first and digests it in another stomach later. Like her, we must also store food before we enjoy food.' Krishna realized why everyone in the village called his cow 'vartaman-Lakshmi', or today's Lakshmi, while his mother was called 'bhavishya-Lakshmi', or tomorrow's Lakshmi. In Dwarka, Satyabhama was Krishna's bhavishya-Lakshmi.

Satyabhama came from a wealthy family and she understood the value of Lakshmi. She knew how to earn, spend, share and save. She took care of Krishna's income as well as his savings. Just as Parvati was Shiva's Mangala, bringing Lakshmi into his home, Satyabhama was Krishna's Mangala, bringing Lakshmi into his home.

| Fresh food for today to enjoy and share | Pickled food to eat and enjoy tomorrow | Seed to plant for the future |

Satyabhama understood that unless we put aside a part of today's Lakshmi, we will never get tomorrow's Lakshmi. If we drink all the cow's milk, there will be no curd for tomorrow, or butter for the day after, or cheese and ghee for the days thereafter. Satyabhama knew the value of savings. That is why she was rich.

When we receive an income, we have to first pay ourselves before we pay others. We pay not our 'current' selves but our 'future' selves. Today we are earning and can therefore afford to pay the bills, repay debts, have fun and be generous. But what happens when we are old and there is no income. We still have to be able to pay the bills, repay debts, have fun and be generous, right? So we need to use our 'current' income to pay our 'future' self.

In Dwarka, Krishna feeds Satyabhama first, before eating. Satyabhama represents Krishna's future. By feeding her, Krishna is feeding his future. He is ensuring there is as much Lakshmi in his future as there is in the present.

The rule of saving is simple: save first, spend later. As soon as you receive any income in hand or in your bank account, put aside 10 per cent or 20 per cent or even 50 per cent towards savings and use the rest to pay the bills, repay debts, have fun and be generous. Saving is actually paying your future self. Always pay yourself first. You owe it to yourself.

How much have you earned?	Is at least 10 per cent of that in your savings?
Last year?	
Last five years?	
Last ten years?	
Since you started work?	

Satyabhama's lesson

We save money only when we spend less than 90 per cent of what we earn. We must save first and then spend. Saving means paying our future selves first. As a young person we must provide for our old self, rather than hope that our children or family will take care of us. That is the responsible thing to do.

6

Why Do We Grab Money?
Kubera on Extortion and Exploitation

Brahma's son, Pulatsya, had a son called Vishrava who in turn had two sons: Kubera and Ravana. Kubera was king of the Yakshas and Ravana was king of the Rakshasas.

In art and religious iconography, Kubera is shown with a pet mongoose who spat jewels. This mongoose killed the Nagas, or serpents, who lived under the earth. He would swallow the Naga-mani, or jewels embedded in the hood of serpents, and spit them out for Kubera. Kubera thus amassed great wealth. He had so much money that his wife came to be known as Nidhi, or treasure. He had nine such wives. Nine Nidhis. He had so much gold that he built a city of gold known as Lanka on the island of Trikuta in the middle of the sea. Kubera had so much food that his stomach grew large until he could no longer walk and had to be carried around by humans. He is the only god whose vahana, or mount, is a human, hence he is called Nara-vahana.

Kubera loved to hoard and did not like to share. This made his brother, Ravana, angry and jealous. Ravana attacked Kubera, threw him out and declared himself king of Lanka. He did to Kubera what Kubera had done to the Nagas. Kubera had killed countless Nagas and grabbed their jewels; Ravana in turn killed Yakshas and grabbed Kubera's golden city of Lanka.

Perhaps the Yakshas and Rakshasas did not know how to exchange. They grabbed what they wanted, just as leaves grab sunlight and the roots grab water, like herbivores eat plants without taking the plant's permission and carnivores eat animals without taking the animal's permission. In nature, grabbing food and killing for food is normal. The Yakshas and Rakshasas killed to steal wealth. Kubera killed the Nagas for their jewels. Ravana drove the Yakshas out to claim their treasures. The Nagas called Kubera a thief. Kubera called Ravana a thief. This cycle of violence mimicked nature's cycle of violence: eat or be eaten. He who kills for food, gets killed to become food.

Rishis sought to help Rakshasas change their

ways—from grabbing to exchanging. But Rakshasas were suspicious of Rishis. They sought Ravana's help to drive Rishis away while Rishis sought the help of Ram to restrain the Rakshasas.

Ravana captured Ram's wife Sita and locked her up in Lanka, determined to make her his queen. She was another man's wife, but Ravana did not care. She resisted, but Ravana did not listen. Ravana's brother, Vibhishana, protested; Ravana simply threw him out of Lanka. Ram, meanwhile, raised an army of monkeys and bears, built a bridge to the island of Rakshasas, attacked Lanka, killed Ravana with the help of Vibhishana and liberated Sita. He installed Vibhishana on the throne of Lanka with the words, 'You helped me defeat Ravana and I repaid my debt by making you king of Lanka. In the same way, you must help others so that they can help you. Never grab; always give to get. This is yagna. This is dharma.'

Those who do not value exchange, exploit, extort

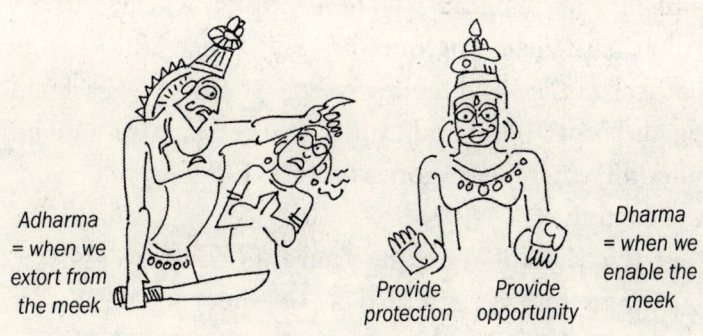

Adharma = when we extort from the meek

Provide protection Provide opportunity

Dharma = when we enable the meek

and steal. In ancient times, warriors would attack farmers and herdsmen to steal their grain and cattle. Later, these warriors claimed the land and turned farmers and herdsmen into slaves, allowing them to live if they gave most of the wealth they generated.

The Vishnu Purana informs us that Rishi Jamadagni got a cow from Kritavirya, king of Haihaiyas, in exchange for his services. Later, the king's son, Kartavirya, wanted the cow back. When Jamadagni resisted, Kartavirya took the cow by force. Furious, Jamadagni's son picked up an axe and hacked Kartavirya to death. Jamadagni's son became famous as Parashuram. Exploitation, extortion and theft always start with violence and end with violence.

In Bhagavata Purana, Krishna is a cowherd and his brother, Balarama, is a herdsman. The two brothers kill Kansa, king of Mathura, and his henchmen, and eventually Kamsa's father-in-law, Jarasandha, king of Magadha, in a wrestling match. This is because Kansa and Jarasandha grab Lakshmi through warfare. They value battlefields, or rana-bhoomi, where the enemy has to be killed and their property plundered. Krishna, on the other hand, values the marketplace, or ranga-bhoomi, where one's goods and services have to delight the customer.

In the Mahabharata, the Kauravas grab the Pandava land and refuse to return it. So the Pandavas take

Parashuram's warning to kings:
You shall not grab.
You shall not allow grabbing.
You shall teach people to exchange.
You shall ensure people repay debts.

the help of Krishna to defeat the Kauravas in war, and reclaim the stolen lands. Krishna then helps the Pandavas appreciate the real role of kings—not to enslave people, exploit their labour and extort their wealth, but to protect their property and create opportunities for yagna. When there is a true Raja (leader), there is no a-raja-kta (anarchy).

Is stealing a crime? These are ethical questions. Consider two scenarios: a poor thief who steals out of hunger and a rich thief who steals in greed. Will you treat the rich thief the same way as you treat a poor thief? Some people would say that nobody should ever steal, no matter the circumstances. Others say if the poor steal, it is okay because they have not been given opportunities. The rich have to use their wealth to create opportunities for others. Stealing (when you have no other option) is not so much the real crime as not creating opportunities (when you have all the resources).

People grab wealth when there are no opportunities. People grab wealth when they do not value exchange. When humans create wealth by plundering resources, they are like the Rakshasas. When humans create wealth by hoarding and not sharing, they are like the Yakshas. A Raja is one who prevents a-raja-kta, where people grab, exploit and extort instead of exchanging. A Kshatriya is one who creates a market full of opportunities.

Tough questions	Answer truthfully
Do you think your boss exploits you or gives you an opportunity for growth?	
Do you think you exploit your maid or cook or driver, or do you give them opportunity for growth?	
If your mother or wife is a home-manager, how is she paid?	
How many jobs have you created?	
Do you see the government as a job creator or tax collector?	

Kubera's lesson
We grab money when we find no opportunities for exchange, or we have no trust in exchange, or when our hunger matters more than other people's hunger.

7

How Do We Manage Money?
Ganesha on Accounting and Planning

Vena was a leader of people who did not respect dharma. He did not conduct yagna. He simply plundered the earth to satisfy his insatiable hunger and made the earth-goddess cry. And so the Rishis took a blade of grass, chanted mantras, and turned it into a missile and killed Vena. Then they took Vena's dead body and crushed it like clay and refashioned a new leader who they named Prithu.

'Will you treat me as a cowherd treats a cow?' asked the earth to the newly created Prithu. Prithu agreed. Earth was Go-mata and he would be Go-pala, the caretaker of the cow. Pleased to hear this, the earth called herself Prithvi—she who is cared for by Prithu.

'What have you spent last year and the year before that?'

'What will you need next year and the year after that?'

Brihaspati reviews past performance

Bhrigu dreams of future possibilities

The earth then took the form of a cow. Rishi Bhrigu told Prithu, 'If you milk the cow, you will be able to feed yourself.' Prithu was about to milk Prithvi when Rishi Brihaspati stopped him. 'Vena hurt the earth and was killed. Don't squeeze Prithvi's udders. She may get hurt and complain and you too may be killed.' So Prithu stopped.

Brihaspati and Bhrigu were rivals. They never agreed on anything. Brihaspati loved the Devas who lived in the sky. Bhrigu preferred the Asuras who lived under the earth. Brihaspati held on to the certainty of the past while Bhrigu projected into the uncertainties of the future. Brihaspati focused on what has already happened, like Vena's death after hurting the earth. Bhrigu showed dreams of how the earth-cow's milk could satisfy all of Prithu's hunger. The two Rishis kept arguing and fighting. Torn between the two advisors, Prithu could not take any decision.

Finally Prithvi told Prithu, 'The problem was not food. The problem was hunger. Vena's hunger was like a wild elephant in heat. He destroyed everything around him to satisfy his hunger. You must have control over your hunger-elephant, so that you can ride it as Indra rides Airavata.'

How could Prithu do that?

Prithvi told Prithu that he would find the answer if he worshipped Ganesha seven times in the ritually prescribed way. 'Make his image in clay, make him offerings of flowers and fruits and fire, and then dissolve his image in water.'

Accordingly, Prithu made the image of Ganesha using clay, made offerings of flowers and fruits and flowers, and then dissolved the image in the river. It was not easy: the image kept falling apart, by the time he found fruits, the flowers had dried up, and while dissolving the image he slipped and fell and sprained his ankle.

The next time, Prithu was able to make the image faster, collect better fruits and flowers and dissolve the image quite easily. The third time, the image was created flawlessly and the worship was meticulous. By the fourth time, the worship could be done on a grand scale.

By the seventh time, Prithu realized something very important: knowledge of the past had helped him plan for the future. Brihaspati maintained records of what had happened during the previous worship and this helped Bhrigu plan the next worship even better.

Past successes and failures informed future actions. Brihaspati could account for how much milk Prithu had consumed in the past, how much he had wasted, the amount of milk that satisfied his hunger and the amount that caused indigestion. Bhrigu could accordingly plan how much milk Prithu should extract from the earth-cow. Brihaspati enabled hindsight. Bhrigu enabled foresight. Prithu made Brihaspati the master of accounting to organize the past and Bhrigu the master of planning to organize the future.

Shiva destroys the hunger-elephant and is therefore called Gajantaka.

During the rituals, Prithu had also observed that Ganesha has the head of an elephant and the body of a man. The head reminded him of the hunger-elephant inside him and the body reminded him of the mahout who tames the wild elephant.

Prithu remembered that Shiva who destroyed Kama was also called Gajantaka, the destroyer of hunger-elephant. Ganesha, as son of Shiva and Parvati, established the middle path of regulating the elephant-hunger, so that we control it and it does not control us.

In Ganesha's hand was an ankush, or elephant goad. The ankush had two parts: a sharp prod that pushes the elephant to move ahead and a hook that pulls the elephant back. Prithu realized the prod is Bhrigu—who thinks of the future. And the hook is Brihaspati—who thinks of the past. On their own, Brihaspati and Bhrigu were useless. The past is gone

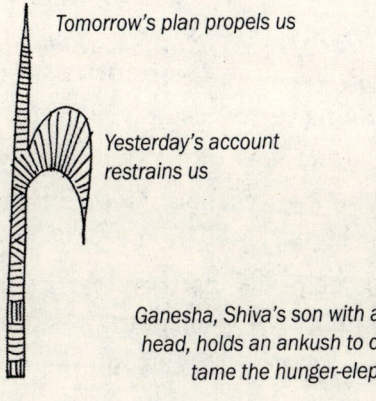

Tomorrow's plan propels us

Yesterday's account restrains us

Ganesha, Shiva's son with an elephant head, holds an ankush to control and tame the hunger-elephant

and the future is yet to come. But in the present, the hook of the past helps to create the prod of the future. Brihaspati can help Bhrigu. Accounting needs to inform planning. Both are important to manage the elephant of hunger so that we control it and it does not control us.

	Brihaspati checklist: Account of last week/ month/year	**Bhrigu checklist: Forecast of current week/month/year**
Earning		
Spending		
Saving		

Prithu told the two advisors, 'Please don't do vi-vaad, and keep arguing about who is better or what is right: that will never solve any problems. Talk to each other, do sam-vaad, let the earth's future be informed by the earth's past and let the past not hold back the future: this will solve many problems.'

Accounting makes us aware of past successes and failures. Planning gives us a vision for the future. Accounting alone has no value unless it informs planning. Planning, without accounting, is wishful thinking, not a goal.

Accounting helps us clarify what is our source of income, how many taxes we pay, how much we spend, share and save. Over time, accounting tells us if our income is rising or falling, if our expenses are rising and falling. Accounting tells us if we are living within our means or living in debt, spending other people's money to satisfy our hunger. Accounting helps us make note of emergency expenses and draws attention to unhealthy spending habits or unused cash.

Expenses	Brihaspati checklist: What did you spend last month?	Bhrigu checklist: What will you spend this month?
Food		
Clothing		
Shelter		
Travel		
Fun		
Debt repayment		
Obligations		
Education		

Planning helps us temper our dreams with reality, and gives us a map for the future. Thanks to accounting, we can calculate predictable expenses and unpredictable expenses—expenses that can be controlled and expenses that cannot be controlled. Planning helps us separate obligatory expenses from aspirational expenses, real income from assumed income, realistic savings from wishful thinking. Accounting helps us budget better for the future. Without planning, we have no clear Sankalpa for yagna.

When people do accounting, they try to do a perfect job. But such a thorough job is for experts and professionals, and at the time of paying taxes. For most of us, on the other hand, being about 90 per cent accurate is sufficient; as long as we broadly understand if we are spending within our means, if our debts are coming down, and if we are saving for the future.

How much will I earn this year?	
How much do I need this year for food, clothing, shelter, travel and utilities?	
How much do I need this year to repay loans to parents or friends or the bank?	
How much do I need this year for holidays and fun?	
How much do you keep aside for emergency or unforeseen expenses?	
How much can I save this year?	

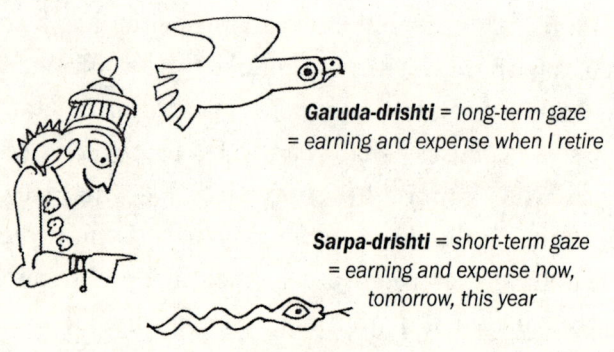

Garuda-drishti = long-term gaze
= earning and expense when I retire

Sarpa-drishti = short-term gaze
= earning and expense now, tomorrow, this year

It is good to compare the Bhrigu checklist (what we planned) with the Brihaspati checklist (what we actually achieved), before creating a new Bhrigu checklist. The future must be informed by the past, in the present.

We can say that Vena was riding an uncontrollable hunger-elephant and so he plundered the earth without any consideration for past or future. Prithu, however, learnt how to tame his hunger-elephant with the help of Brihaspati and Bhrigu. Accounting of the past and planning of the future are the two interdependent tools that help us manage money. To remind us of the value of hindsight and foresight, Brihaspati and Bhrigu, two elephants are always found next to Lakshmi, raising their trunks and pouring water on her.

Expenses you foresee five years from now	Expenses you foresee ten years from now	Expenses you foresee twenty years from now	Expenses you foresee forty years from now

Accounting and planning need to be both short term and long term. What did we do in the past to achieve long-term goals and balance it with decisions to achieve long-term goals. This helps us determine how we plan saving and spending in the future: short term and long term. To think short term and be tactical about what our plans in the previous or current year is to think like having a snake's narrow vision, hence called Sarpa-drishti. To think long term and be strategic about old investments years and so planning for retirement is like having a bird's wide vision, hence called Garuda-drishti.

Ganesha's lesson
Accounting and planning are key activities for managing money. Only accounting without planning stops us from thinking long term. Only planning without accounting prevents successful implementation.

8

Why Can We Never Avoid Taxes?
Shukra on Fairness

Brahma's son, Marichi, had a son called Kashyapa who had two wives, Aditi and Diti. The sons of Aditi were called Devas and they lived in the sky. The sons of Diti were called Asuras and they lived under the earth.

The Devas were hungry. Brahma told them to churn the ocean of milk. Meru, the king of mountains, served as the churning rod. It was kept on the back of Akupara, the king of turtles, to keep it afloat. Vasuki, the king of serpents, coiled around Meru to serve as the churning rope.

The Devas held the tail-end of the serpent and served as the force of the churn. They asked their half-brothers, the Asuras, who lived under the earth, to hold the other end of the serpent rope, and serve as the counter-force. The Asuras agreed because they were hungry too.

The ocean was churned for hundreds and hundreds of years. The coiling and uncoiling made Vasuki vomit poison. The Devas asked Shiva to drink it as only Shiva had the power to digest poison. Slowly the treasures of the ocean of milk emerged like butter. Trees, cows, gems and pots that fulfilled every desire and ushered in prosperity came forth. Music, song, dance, art and wine that brought pleasure were born. Elephants, horses, weapons and medicines that gave power appeared.

Then came amrita, the nectar of immortality. The Devas drank it first. This made them immortal. They killed the Asuras and took everything with them and created Swarga.

Shukra, advisor and coach of the Asuras, was upset at the unfairness displayed by the Devas. He knew the secret of reviving the dead: Sanjivani Vidya. So he brought the dead Asuras back to life. He taught them how to get boons from Brahma and use them to grab from Swarga their rightful share. The Asuras, however, were not content with taking their share; they would take everything, just as the Devas had.

The Devas fought back, led by Indra. When they won, they too claimed everything, and pushed the

Who decides what your share is?

Asuras back to Patala, their realm below the earth. Neither believed in sharing. Neither really understood the purpose of yagna.

In Ramayana, brothers Vali and Sugriva fight over the monkey kingdom of Kishkinda, and in Mahabharata, Pandavas and Kauravas fight over Kuru-kshetra. In all these cases, either one or both parties do not care for the other's hunger. They mimic the eternal unending battles of the Devas and the Asuras, the entitled and the deprived.

Sometimes the Asuras won. Sometimes they lost. But neither victory nor defeat was permanent. With Shukra's help, the Asuras came back again and again

Recipe for quarrels:

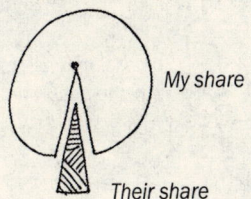

My share
Their share

Bhagavan is the one who is wise enough to make the cut (bhag) and give the share (bhaag) that makes all parties happy.

Devdutt Pattanaik

and laid siege to Swarga. Thus, the Devas who had all the prosperity, pleasure and power in the world, never had peace.

(NOTE: Devas are not 'gods' and Asuras are not 'demons'. In the Puranas, Asuras are not seen as evil or morally wrong.)

Asuras are the half-brothers of Devas. Both descend from Brahma. Both are fighting over Lakshmi, which both churned from the ocean of milk. The Devas feel it was their initiative and enterprise too, and so they are entitled to her. The Asuras feel they deserve a fair share, because they collaborated, and because they are half-brothers, with as much right on the ocean of milk (earth) and its treasures (Lakshmi), as the Devas.

Capitalists will side with the Devas: it was their enterprise, their idea, so they decide what is fair pay. Communists with the Asuras: it was their labour that made the enterprise successful and so they deserve more pay. Rishis will simply see a failure of yagna, the refusal of the Devas to empathize with the hunger

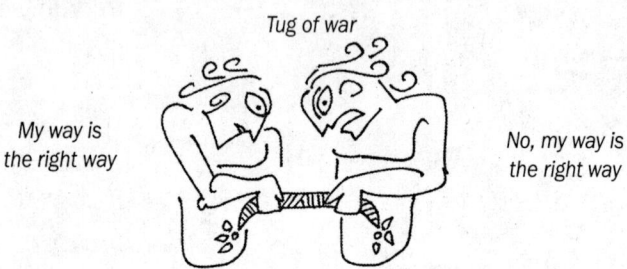

Tug of war

My way is the right way

No, my way is the right way

Manthan = churning

When you give, I receive.

When you pull, I pause.

When I speak, you listen.

When I give, you receive.

When I pause, you pull.

When I listen, you speak.

of the Asuras. They argue about what is right and so are engaged in tug of war, as lawyers in a court of law. They are not focused on acknowledging the interdependence of both their hungers, which is what churning is all about.

(NOTE: Deva and Devata are not the same thing. The Devas, like the Asuras, are children of Brahma. Both can perform yagna and invoke the Devata, and they both do.)

During the yagna of churning of the ocean of milk, the Devas are the Yajaman and the Asuras are the Devata. As Yajaman, the Devas had nothing to give except promises. They convinced the Asuras to give them the service they required. But when the fruits of the labour emerged, the Devas did not give a share to the Asuras. So the Devas are in Hrinn. They owe the Asuras. The Asuras attack to claim their share of the yagna. They see this as justice. The Devas reject the Asura claim. The result is war. Relentless war, between the Asuras who are fighting for what they feel is rightfully theirs, and the Devas who feel they owe no one anything. The Devas did not complete the transaction. The yagna is incomplete. They remain in debt. Hence, they have prosperity but no peace.

(NOTE: Asuras and Rakshasas are not the same thing, though most people today use the terms interchangeably, as both are feared.)

Rakshasas fight Rishis and Asuras fight Devas. Rakshasas fight Rishis because they only know to grab food and have not yet learnt to exchange goods and services. Rakshasas prefer the forest to the market. Asuras fight Devas because they have been cheated during exchange and so have stopped trusting the yagna. They feel tricked and exploited by the market.

Taxes	What do you pay?
Tax on expenses (goods and services)	
Tax on income	
Tax on savings	
Tax on investment	
Tax on inheritance	

The ocean of milk symbolizes the earth as well as the market. Industries 'churn' plant wealth, animal wealth, mineral wealth. Buyers and sellers 'churn' goods and services in markets. There are Devas whose initiative establishes the churn, and Asuras without whom the churn cannot function. Neither the earth nor the market belongs to the Devas or the Asuras. So the Devas cannot corner all the Lakshmi. She must be shared with everyone. Otherwise, there will be hunger, and hunger leads to war.

In dharma, a king taxes the rich to create opportunties for the poor as well as services for all. In adharma, a king taxes the rich for his own pleasure, or taxes the poor to favour the rich, or does not use it for public good. Taxes are people's money to be spent on people. King and government are mere custodians who make this happen. They are service providers, not masters or owners. The tax is not theirs to keep.

Public expenses	What do you think your taxes pay for?
Salaries and pension of government	
Public roads and railways	
Public schools	
Public hospitals	
Public toilets	
Subsidies to poor	

Taxes are the debt that the Devas owe Asuras. We cannot escape taxes. Every time there is income, taxes return, like Asuras attacking Swarga again and again. No one likes taxes. We pay them grudgingly.

We feel Asuras do not deserve a share of our wealth, or at least the share they claim. But if taxes are not paid, what will our brothers eat? If they churn for Lakshmi themselves, then they stop being Asuras; they become Devas too. And they will be taxed too.

Shukra's lesson
We cannot avoid taxes as long as we share the earth with other people, and as long as we cannot give food away voluntarily to those who cannot feed themselves and others.

9

How Do We Guard Wealth?
Hanuman on Insurance and Will

During the war between Ram and Ravana on the shores of Lanka, Lakshman was fatally injured but luckily there was Hanuman who managed to fly across the sea and carry back the mountain on which grew the Sanjivani herb that brought Lakshman back to life. Hanuman saved the day. Under his protection, everyone was safe.

Hanuman learnt that Ravana had enlisted the help of Mahiravan, king of Patala, to abduct Ram. So Hanuman extended his mighty tail and coiled it around Ram to create an impregnable fort. That way no one could reach Ram.

But Hanuman forgot that Patala is located under

the earth. Mahiravan simply dug a hole from below to reach Ram, while Hanuman's tail protected Ram from threats above. When Hanuman uncoiled his tail, he saw to his dismay the hole leading to Patala through which Ram had been taken. He immediately plunged in and after many adventures managed to rescue Ram and bring him back to the surface of the earth.

Hanuman was upset that Mahiravan had breached his security ring. Ram then told Hanuman, 'Don't you know that nothing in this world is perfect or absolute. Everything has a weakness. Every Asura does tapasya to secure immortality from Brahma but that is one boon no one can give. So Asuras come up with clever demands like "no man can kill me", or "I should die neither at day nor at night", creating conditions that help them bypass death. But the Asuras end up being outsmarted always: the Asura who no man could kill was killed by a woman, the Asura who could not be killed at day or at night was killed at twilight which is neither day nor night. Life is full of risks, some predictable, some unpredictable. My father had four sons hoping that one of them would be around when he was dying. Yet when he died, two of his sons were in the forest, and two others were in their uncle's house. My father knew he would some day die, but he could not predict when he would die. Risks thus are always predictable and unpredictable. Hanuman, you

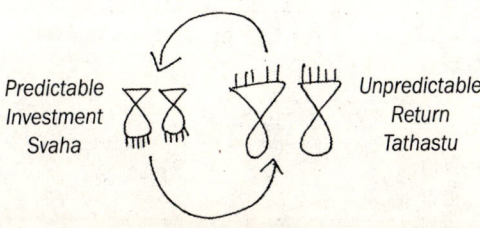

No guarantees in life

predicted risk from above the earth and coiled your tail around me. But you could not predict the underground tunnel from Patala. But you still managed to save the day, by going to Patala and overpowering Mahiravan. This is what life is about, managing predictability and being prepared for unpredictability.'

There are emergencies in life that are expected—health issues, accidents, death, damage to property by fire or theft or vandalism. But we never know when any of these might happen, or how bad it will be. Accidents are predictable but their timing and intensity is unpredictable. That is why we need to insure ourselves.

Insurance is a strange yagna: it is investment that gives us returns only when things go wrong. Insurance is the money we lose or the price we pay when nothing goes wrong, when there are no emergencies. Insurance is the benefit we get only when things go bad.

The smart man focuses on maintaining the stability of good times rather than being hungry for a return on money deposited for insurance.

Predictable calamities	How do you guard yourself?
Hospitalization	
Accident of vehicle	
Death and resulting loss of income to spouse and children	
Theft/fire at home/office	
Children fighting over property after parents' death	

We lose money in health insurance if we stay healthy, and we get money from health insurance if we fall sick. The smart person focuses on maintaining health, not 'losing' money. This is health insurance.

We lose money in general insurance if our house does not catch fire but we get money from general insurance if our house catches fire. The smart person focuses on not letting their house catch fire, rather than on 'losing' money.

Insurance:

If ship returns, money is mine.

If house is safe, money is mine.

If you are healthy, money is mine.

If there is no accident, money is mine.

When you are alive, money is mine.

If ship sinks, money is yours.

If house catches fire, money is yours.

If you are sick, money is yours.

If there is accident, money is yours.

When you die, money is your family's.

We don't make any money on life insurance but our family members do upon our death. The smart man focuses on the money his family will get after his death, rather than money he is 'losing' when he is alive.

Many years after Ram had ruled Ayodhya, it was time for him to return to Vaikuntha. For this, he had to first die. But Yama, god of death, could not enter Ayodhya, as Hanuman would not let him in. Hanuman feared that without Ram, the whole city would collapse. So Ram asked Hanuman, 'What is the most amazing thing in the world?' Hanuman had no answer. Ram revealed to him, 'Everyday people fall sick, houses get burnt and people die, yet the healthy never think they will get sick, the residents never think their homes will catch fire, and the living refuse to believe they will die. The day I was born I knew I would die. I was prepared for accidents and calamities and emergencies. My brothers were my insurance for Ayodhya when I was exiled to the forest. My children are my insurance for Ayodhya when I leave for Vaikuntha. My father's will was known to all and so we brothers did not fight in the way the Asuras fight the Devas. My will is also known to all, so my children will not fight like the Asuras fight the Devas.' Hanuman learnt his lesson and allowed Yama to enter Ayodhya.

But many people feel that if they think about death and misfortune, they will attract death and misfortune.

Prepare your will when you are alive.

The dead cannot communicate their will to the living.

They avoid discussing accidents, emergencies, calamities and death. Hence they avoid talking about insurance. And they never talk about their will while they are alive. They focus on life and amassing a fortune, in the hope that they will delay death and avoid misfortune. When accidents happen, they regret not insuring themselves. When children fight over property, they blame parents for not making a will. But it is too late.

Understanding the past makes us realistic about the future, neither too optimistic or too pessimistic. This is called sama-chitta-bhava, or equanimity. It helps in buying insurance regularly, and preparing as well as updating wills.

Hanuman's lesson
When we are alive, we guard wealth by insuring ourselves against predictable and unpredictable risks. When we are dead, we guard our wealth only if we have prepared a clear will when alive.

10

How Do We Attract Money?
Vishnu on Repeat Orders and Referrals

Hanuman is a popular god because he is sankat-mochan, or the problem-solver. Ganesha is a popular god because he is vighna-harta, or the obstacle-remover. There are thousands of temples in India: in every corner of every city, in homes, on roads, next to stations, in marketplaces, in business establishments. People go there to solve problems, to remove obstacles, to get boons, or simply for peace of mind.

But some temples are more popular than others, even if they are located in faraway mountains. These temples are very popular because people who go there feel their wishes will surely be fulfilled. These are known as 'ichha-purti' (wish-fulfilling) temples.

Among the most acknowledged ichha-purti temples are the Tirupati Balaji Temple in Andhra Pradesh, Jagannath Puri in Odisha, and Nathdvara in Rajasthan. These are Vishnu temples.

Both Vishnu and Indra are Devatas but there are more temples to Vishnu and almost none to Indra. Vishnu is the Devata who focuses on giving more than getting, unlike Indra who focuses more on getting than giving. So there are more temples to Vishnu than Indra.

Indra is constantly fighting battles with Rajas and Tapasvis and Asuras for securing his Swarga. Vishnu is constantly doing leela to delight those who call him. Indra is in the battlefield, or rana-bhoomi, seeking to capture and plunder Lakshmi, while Vishnu on the performing stage, or ranga-bhoomi, delighting Lakshmi. We always prefer going to a ranga-bhoomi, where we feel nourished, than a battlefield where we are drained and exploited.

When we like a performance, we go back to see it. Likewise, we go back to a temple when our wishes are fulfilled after praying there. We never go empty handed. We always go bearing gifts—flowers, fruits, light, flags, perfume and fabric, even song and dance. If a temple gives us peace of mind, we go back there again and again. This is called repeat order.

Any business in life is successful when it gets repeat orders. Let's say there is a shop that sells all the things you want. You went to the shop for the first time, because you wanted to buy rare fruits like kiwi or dragon fruit. The shopkeeper supplied you with the kiwi and dragon fruit. Next time you want these exotic fruits, you will go back to the same shop. In fact, when you go back repeatedly to the shop, the shopkeeper feels happy because he has got many orders from you, and might therefore even give you a discount, which makes you value the shop more. He makes money; your wishes are fulfilled. You keep going again and again. Repeat order.

The same is true of a friend. You make a friend and you go back to a friend when they satisfy your wishes. They are good to talk to, they give you positive energy and when you are low they pick you up. They give you good advice, they are there with you, they give you emotional support. You want their company again and again. You avoid friends who make you feel negative and small. You seek company that makes you feel positive and big. So basically, those who fulfil our wishes are always desired and we give them repeat orders.

When I keep getting satisfied repeatedly, I tell other people about these temples—my uncle, my aunt, my friend, my niece, my nephew, my spouse and my child. This is called referral. Just like you introduce your shopkeeper and your friends to your family and other friends. The more the referral, the bigger are the orders and the more the success. Because those referred can also give further orders, and if satisfied, more referrals. Think of that small shop in a small town that makes a tasty chaat, which everyone likes. People go there repeatedly. They take their friends along. The friends then go repeatedly and tell more friends. Thus the small shop in the small town becomes famous, and makes a lot of money, without any marketing or advertising.

On your mobile phone, you need good connectivity, so every telecom company says it will satisfy your wish. You experiment, you try them out and when they satisfy your wishes, you become a loyal customer, seeking their service again and again and paying them again and again. When you are very happy, you spread the word and tell others to join the network you have found best and that is how a telecom company attracts more and more customers and becomes truly successful.

Your goods or service provider	That you have ordered from more than once	That you have recommended to others

I came again as I was happy the last time with these goods and services.

I came because trustworthy folks recommended these goods and services.

The unique thing about Hindu temples is that they are VOLUNTARY. You are not obliged to go to a Hindu temple. You go to temples when you want, if you want, if you feel you get positive energy or your wishes are being fulfilled, or you get some other benefit from the temple. Otherwise, you do not go. In other words, this is a free market; nobody holds you back, nobody forces you. So a temple's success is not based on rules or laws, but the genuine trust of people, making them visit again and again, and getting more people with them.

To be successful and make money in life, we should delight our customers, no matter what goods or services we provide. We must do it consistently so that we get repeat orders from old customers and clients and we are constantly referred to other new customers and clients. Successful temples are those temples where people come voluntarily. Customers prefer coming to the ranga-bhoomi where they are delighted with goods and services, over the rana-bhoomi where they have to constantly fight to get what they want.

When we delight the Yajaman, the Yajaman keeps calling us repeatedly to his yagna. He also tells others to invite us to their yagna. The more Tathastu we give, the more popular we are, the more trusted we are and the more Svaha we get.

List reasons why people seek you out	If they had another choice, would you still be sought?	Can that make you money?

Vishnu's lesson
We attract money when we delight our customer with our goods and services so much that they keep coming back, and they even recommend us to others. This is the opposite of grabbing money by cheating the system, tricking the market and exploiting employees.

11

How Do We Share Money?
Varuna on Charity and Investment

A small fish came to Manu, the first human, and begged him to save him from the big fish who wanted to eat him. Manu put the fish in a pot of water. Next day the fish grew in size. To survive, he needed more water. And so Manu put him in a larger pot. The fish kept growing, and Manu kept giving the fish larger and larger pots, until it became so big that it had to be put in a pond, a lake, a river, and eventually back in the sea. Manu hoped that the sea would swell so that the fish had enough to eat. To his horror this was exactly what happened. It kept raining and the oceans began to swell, consuming the land.

Manu had no place to go. He built a ship to

prevent himself from drowning. Then suddenly he saw a gigantic fish appear from nowhere. This fish, or matsya, towed Manu's boat to the highest peak in the world—Meru.

We cannot satisfy everyone's hunger as human hunger is insatiable. Unlike animals who eat when hungry and don't eat when they're not hungry, humans are hungry all the time. We imagine future hunger and so we are never satisfied. Also, society encourages us to be dissatisfied and aspire for more. We are told to be ambitious. Often, ambition is another word for greed. Like the fish, we keep seeking more and more food. And if Manu is feeding us, why would we learn to feed ourselves. It is easier to get food than to find food, grab food or earn food. Manu needs to realize when to stop giving. Manu needs to help the fish become independent and dependable, not dependent. That is true charity. That is daan.

Varuna, god of sea, is famous for his charity. He gives his daughter Lakshmi to the world in the form of freshwater rains to quench everyone's thirst. But we never think we owe the sea anything. Because the sea asks nothing in return. No matter how much water we use, the sea does not shrink in size or become dry. Eventually, water returns to the sea in the form of rivers. The incoming rivers do not cause the sea to swell because the sea never takes more than it has given.

Varuna is content—neither depleting with rains, nor expanding with rivers. Varuna's charity is part of an exchange: he knows that what he gives as rain eventually will return as rivers. He feeds those who eventually learn to feed themselves and others, who in turn do the same, until eventually all food returns to him. This charity as part of exchange is daan. It makes people independent and dependable.

Neither the Devas nor the Asuras follow daan.

Devas give dakshina: they feed those who have fed them. In other words, Devas prefer exchange over charity. They value other people's hunger only when their hunger is satisfied. They do not like being trapped in debt or entrapping others in debt. They depend on those who depend on them. Thus, there is reciprocity and interdependence.

Asuras give bhiksha—they feed without asking anything in exchange. They prefer charity and welfare over exchange. Asuras make the hungry dependent on them and indebted to them.

Bali, the Asura, rejected yagna because he saw how the Devas had tricked the Asuras of their share during the churning of the ocean of milk. Since the Devas did not give the Asuras the promised share, Bali decided to take everything that the Devas had by force. He attacked Swarga, drove Indra out and claimed Lakshmi for himself.

Now everyone with any aspiration or obligation had to come to Bali, as all wealth was with him. Bali gave wealth freely. As ruler of the realms above and below the earth, he declared that he would satisfy everyone's desires. Everyone who came to him got whatever they wanted, and so everyone was happy with his rule. Everyone forgot Indra.

Indra had a brother called Vishnu. It was he who had taken the form of a fish to teach Manu about the dangers of charity without exchange. He took the form of a dwarf, or Vaman, to teach Bali the same lesson.

He approached Bali and asked for three paces of land, meaning land that he could cover in three steps. Looking at his size, Bali concluded that this would amount to very little land. 'Sure you don't want more?' he asked. Vaman said no. Vaman checked, 'Will I be in your debt if you give me land?' Bali said no, for he believed in charity and welfare, not exchange.

As soon as Bali granted the three paces of land to him, Vaman transformed into a giant and took two steps: with one he covered the world above the earth and with the other he covered the world below the earth. 'Where do I take my third step?' asked the dwarf-turned-giant. 'Before you answer. Hear this story.'

This is the story Vaman told Bali: 'One day, Kubera, god of treasures, came to Mount Kailas to meet Shiva and realized there is no food there. He saw Shiva's

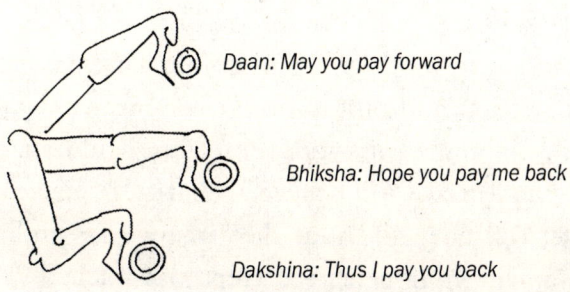

Daan: May you pay forward

Bhiksha: Hope you pay me back

Dakshina: Thus I pay you back

son, the pot-bellied Ganesha, and felt sorry for him. Clearly, he loved food but had a father who did not provide any. So he invited Ganesha to eat in his house to his heart's content. Ganesha accepted the invitation, went to Kubera's house and kept eating. He ate and ate and ate, until all of Kubera's treasures were exhausted. A poor Kubera begged Ganesha to stop. Ganesha stopped and told Kubera that human hunger is insatiable. The more food humans get, the more insecure they get; they want to hoard more food. Need gives way to greed. But they call greed "ambition" and fool themselves. No one can satisfy everyone's hunger. Hence, he who feeds, must demand to be fed.'

Realization dawned on Bali upon hearing this story. Dwarf-hunger became giant-hunger and even the three worlds were consumed by two paces of land, leaving the receiver dissatisfied as it was one-pace short. No one can satisfy other people's hunger. Hunger keeps increasing over time until it outstrips the supply of food. It is not enough to make food available. Ironically, access to food ignites more hunger than it satisfies. It is also important to outgrow hunger. 'Step on my head. Claim me with your third step,' said Bali.

Vaman was pleased. 'You believe in charity. I believe in exchange. You have given me the three worlds and yourself. I am in your debt. So I repay my debt by serving as your doorman—reminding those who visit you that unless they give, they cannot get, and if they get without giving, they will always be in your debt.'

As long as we are hungry, we will hate feeding others. That is why we hate taxes and avoid charity. Unless there is contentment, taxes will never be paid joyfully and charity will never be done voluntarily. In the absence of contentment, taxes are forced using ideas like 'social justice' and charity is demanded using ideas like 'social responsibility'.

Insecure Indra

Tax is dakshina we are forced to give in order to repay our debt to society. Charity is bhiksha that puts the hungry in our debt, makes them increasingly dependent on us, and we feel increasingly entrapped. We hope our bhiksha will make our lives better and keep the hungry away; but they keep coming back and we get increasingly exasperated and irritated by their demands. Neither tax nor charity is daan.

Daan is a wise, long-term investment without any expectation of any returns. It is done with the faith that our money enables many, not all, to uplift themselves (uddhaar) so that they can in turn uplift many others. In daan, our money eventually returns to us in a different form: as a peaceful, prosperous and civilized world, just as water that leaves the sea as rain, returns to the sea as rivers.

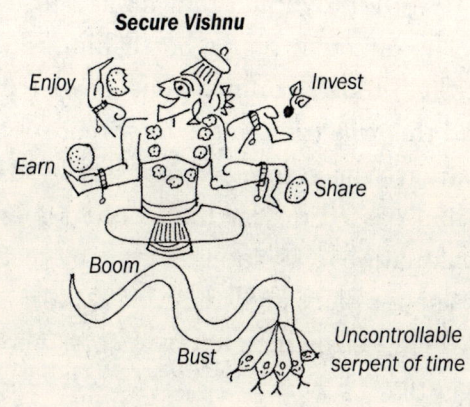

Dakshina: List all the repayments you do in your life for goods and services received, out of a sense of gratitude or obligation	Bhiksha: List all the charity and welfare activities you do in life without expecting anything in return except spiritual merit and legacy	Daan: List all the activities you do to make other people independent and dependable rather than dependent

Vaman explained to Bali the difference between bhiksha and daan by narrating the story of Indradyumna. Indradyumna had donated many cows in his lifetime. As a result he accumulated a lot of merit and so obtained a place in Swarga. There he lived in luxury with Indra for hundreds of years. Then one day Indra told Indradyumna that he had to leave Swarga as no one on earth remembered him donating cows. A shocked Indradyumna went down to earth and realized this was true: in the hundreds of years he was in Swarga, where time passes slowly, thousands of years had passed on earth. No one remembered him or his donations. 'As soon as your merit is forgotten, you lose your place in Swarga,' said Indra. 'If you wish to stay here longer, then find someone who remembers your charity.'

Indradyumna searched the world and no one remembered him. He asked the oldest sage, Markandeya, who asked the oldest crow, Kakabhusandi, who directed him to the oldest tortoise, Akupara. Akupara said, 'Yes, I remember Indradyumna. He made the pond where I live.' But Indradyumna had never built a pond in his life. So he was confused. Then Akupara explained. 'When you donated cows, they would kick up dust as they were leaving your cowshed. You gave so many cows who kicked up so much dust that a depression formed in front of your cowshed. Here, water accumulated during the rains and it became a pond where plants grew and animals thrived: fishes, frogs, geese, snakes and tortoise. I am the grandson of one such tortoise. And we call ourselves the tortoise who belong to Indradyumna's pond.'

Indradyumna told Indra about how the tortoise in

the pond remembered him for the good deed he did not even know he had done. Indra smiled and let Indradyumna stay in Swarga for as long as the tortoise identified Indradyumna's pond as their home.

On hearing this, Bali realized how voluntary but self-conscious, result-oriented donations are bhiksha. Here the focus is fame and legacy as Tathastu. We want our names carved in stone on the walls of the schools and hospitals and roads we build. They grant us fame and legacy for a limited period of time, as long as we are remembered. Daan is generosity born of detachment, done without being self-conscious, and without knowing or seeking any outcome or recognition—by focussing on Svaha alone.

Varuna's lesson

We can share wealth by paying our bills, by repaying our debts, by paying taxes. In most cases, we share wealth grudgingly, because we are expected to. Sometimes we share wealth with expectations and conditions attached, hoping to change the world, or be remembered for our good deeds. But true sharing is giving money where the returns are not measurable or guaranteed, to feed the other without concern for the self.

12

How Do We Grow Money?
Shakambari on Debt and Equity

What makes Swarga qualify as paradise? In Swarga, there are trees known as Kalpavrikshas that fulfil your dreams. Just ask and the tree will bear fruit. There are cows that fulfil your wishes and they are called Kamadhenus. The rocks and the pebbles also give you whatever you want or need, which is why they are all called Chintamani. Every pot and pan in Swarga is overflowing with grain and gold. The contents never diminish or empty, no matter how much you take from the pots and pans, which is why they are called Akshay Patra. Imagine going to an ATM machine and taking out ₹5,000 and discovering that the money is getting replaced automatically. Imagine there is always money in your ATM, no matter how much you spend, even if you earn nothing or do no work. Wouldn't that be amazing? That is what Swarga is.

Providing goods and services gives us income. To make income sustainable, we have to ensure we are always above competition, always in demand, always relevant, valued and trusted enough to obtain repeat order and referrals. A sustainable income takes care of all our bills. With our excess wealth, we can have fun. With our excess wealth we can build assets such as property and land and gold; we feel rich, we feel like Indra in Swarga.

This is labh (profit). Not shubh-labh (profit with peace).

There is no peace in Swarga because Swarga is surrounded by hunger—the hunger of Asuras, Rakshasas

Labh: Profit without Joy   **Shubh-Labh:** Profit with Joy

and Pisachas, those who feel we owe them their share of food, those who do not know how to exchange but only to steal, and those who want food but cannot feed. People want to steal our money, our gold, encroach our land, steal our property. We are always scared of loss. Life becomes a stress-filled war zone.

To create profit with peace, for shubh-labh, we have to learn from Vishnu whose heaven is Vaikuntha. Vishnu's couch is essentially the coils of a serpent floating on the ocean of milk. Yet, he is never insecure. While Indra's throne wobbles, Vishnu's enjoys the swing provided by the rising and falling waves. In other words, Indra fears the loss of Lakshmi and clings to her. Vishnu enjoys giving Lakshmi away and she always comes back to him, exponentially.

Unlike Indra who thinks only of his hunger, Vishnu thinks of the hunger of all beings, Asuras included. He does not fear those outside Vaikuntha. Instead, he serves their interests. He sees everyone as part of his family who he has to feed until they grow up to feed themselves and others. He genuinely believes the world is his family—Vasudhaiva Kutumbakam. Some relatives are positive. Some are negative. But he works for everyone's upliftment (uddhar), which means feeding the hungry until they can feed themselves and others, and eventually him. The more people he feeds, the more people feed him back. The more people he helps in finding food, the more people provide him with food.

Indra fears he will lose the fruits of Swarga to others. Vishnu is more than happy giving away the fruit of Vaikuntha. Lakshmi goes down to the earth, and Vishnu follows her to ensure people treat her well. They eat the fruit and plant the seed too, so that a tree grows that bears more fruit, which more people can eat and share with him. The more people he gives fruit to, the more people get fed, the more people grow plants, the more people have fruit-bearing trees that they share with him. Thus, he creates a virtuous cycle—where he gives Lakshmi and ends up getting Lakshmi. In Vishnu's yagna, the Sankalpa is to not to make himself prosperous; his Sankalpa is to make the Devata prosperous.

For Indra, only his own happiness matters. For Vishnu, the happiness of others makes him happy. So Indra pursues labh while Vishnu pursues shubh-labh. Indra chases Lakshmi as a tiger chases a deer; the deer

Rana-bhoomi:
I am afraid Lakshmi will be taken away from me because I invest only in myself.

Ranga-bhoomi:
I am confident Lakshmi will come to me because I always invest in others for myself.

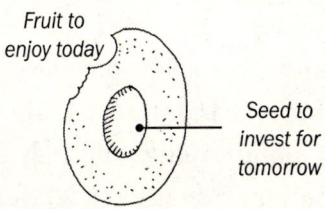

Income has two parts:
Income is both fruit (phala) and seed (bija). In Gita, Krishna says that we must focus on action (planting seed) not on results (harvesting fruit).

Fruit to enjoy today

Seed to invest for tomorrow

must die for Indra's hunger to be satisfied. Vishnu attracts Lakshmi as a flower attracts a bee; the bee helps the flower transform into a fruit, which contains the seed of another tree that can produce more flowers that can provide more nectar to bees. So the cycle continues.

How do we create a Vaikuntha where Lakshmi given, returns manifold? We do this when we look at our income as fruit (phala) and seed (bija). Fruit is the money used to pay bills, repay debts and buy property. Seed is the money used to invest for the future, to help ourselves by helping others.

We can help others by lending them money or by investing in their business. With our extra money we can be moneylenders or shareholders. Lenders expect money that was borrowed to be returned with interest. This is making money through debt. Shareholders have a stake in the enterprise and expect a share of the business profit. This is making money through equity. Debt is low-risk but low-return. Equity is high-risk but high-return.

Either we directly become moneylenders or business partners, or we can outsource this to banks and financial institutions, who will invest in debt-funds and equity-funds on our behalf, working towards minimum risk and maximum return in each case by lending to, or investing in, multiple companies, in multiple industries, after careful consideration.

Just as seeds take a long time to germinate and transform into fruit-bearing trees, investments take a long time to give returns. But we tend to be impatient. We want high returns now! And we want high returns all the time. And that creates a problem. We learn this in the story of three yoginis: Vimala, Nirmala and Kamala. These three yoginis were given a golden fruit by Lakshmi.

The first yogini named Vimala ate the golden fruit and swallowed the golden seed. The next day she was

Investments demand patience

How long must I wait till the seed becomes a tree?

Should I cut the tree and sell the wood, or wait for the fruits?

once again hungry, so she went looking for another fruit.

The second yogini, Nirmala, ate the golden fruit and planted the seed. She waited for the plant to grow and bear golden fruit. But she got impatient after two years when the tree did not bear fruit. She cut the tree and gave its golden wood to a carpenter, in exchange for a large quantity of regular fruit that satisfied her hunger; but only for a year.

The third yogini, Kamala, ate the golden fruit, planted the golden seed and waited patiently for the tree to grow and bear golden fruit. It happened in the third year. The tree bore a hundred golden fruits. The third yogini had learnt the value of patience.

Kamala ate the hundred golden fruits and sowed a hundred seeds again. Three years later, fifty of them gave fifty golden fruits each. So she had 2,500 golden fruits and as many seeds. She had learnt about exponential growth: every seed has the potential of several fruits, each of which contains a seed.

But then a drought struck. The trees did not bear fruit one year. The third yogini feared the next year there would be drought too and the golden-fruit bearing trees would wither away. Should she cut the golden wood and sell it to carpenters before the wood got bad? But what if there was no drought? Not sure, she cut half the trees and sold their wood in exchange

I planted this when my age was	20	30	40	50
To be enjoyed when my age will be	50	60	70	80

for fruit for the year. The next year, there was no drought. The remaining trees once again bore golden fruit and she heaved a sigh of relief. She had learnt to take risks cautiously.

In the following years, some golden fruits Kamala ate and enjoyed, never forgetting to sow the seeds. Some fruits were stolen by Rakshasas who did not know any better. This was theft that she wrote off. Some fruits she had to give to the Asuras who felt her garden had destroyed the forest they hunted in and so she owed them food. This was tax. It ensured the Asuras did not attack her. In fact, they protected her. Some she gave to the Pisachas, who were always hungry but could never give anything in exchange.

*Giving loans to people and businesses (**debt-fund**): Promise to return four fruits after one year*

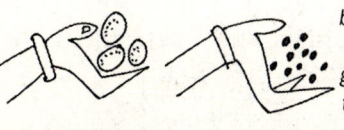

*Buying shares in business (**equity-fund**): If seeds germinate, half of the trees and the fruits they bear belong to me*

Kamala never forgot her sisters, Vimala and Nirmala. She gave Vimala a golden fruit, for taking care of her when she was sick. This was dakshina, exchange. She gave Nirmala seeds, without seeking anything in return, and told her how to be patient till the trees bore fruit. This was daan, for it helped Vimala become independent.

While Vimala's tree was growing, Vimala would borrow golden fruits from Kamala, with the promise to return the same number of fruits with an extra one, when her tree bore fruit. Lending gave Kamala the assured returns of one extra fruit, with little risk.

While Nirmala's tree was growing, Kamala told Nirmala to give her some more fruits. 'I will eat the fruit and plant the seed and take care of the planted seed. If the seeds grow and bear fruit, half the output will be yours. But if they don't grow or bear fruit, I will give you nothing.' This was a great risk, but the returns were much more compared to the loan she had given to Vimala. Investing gave Kamala the promise of more fruits, but at greater risk.

The interest paid by Vimala on the loans she had taken from Kamala and the profit shared by Nirmala for the equity Kamala bought ensured Kamala got fruit without having to plant seeds in her own garden and taking care of them. Each fruit she received, she reinvested as a loan or equity. Others did this for her. So she kept getting more and more golden fruits, each containing a golden seed, which kept bearing more golden fruits containing golden seeds.

Eventually, Kamala came to be known as Shakambari, the goddess of fruits and seeds and trees, who feeds herself by feeding others. She had learnt how to be Vishnu and make Lakshmi keep coming her way again and again and again with minimum effort, not losing heart during the bad times, and taking full advantage of the good times.

Where can money be used as seed to bear fruit on its own?	Per cent of your savings	Risk rank*	Return rank*
Savings account		6	6
Fixed deposit		5	5
Debt fund (lending)		4	4
Gold		3	3
Property		2	2
Equity fund (shares, stocks)		1	1

*1 = Maximum and 6 = Minimum

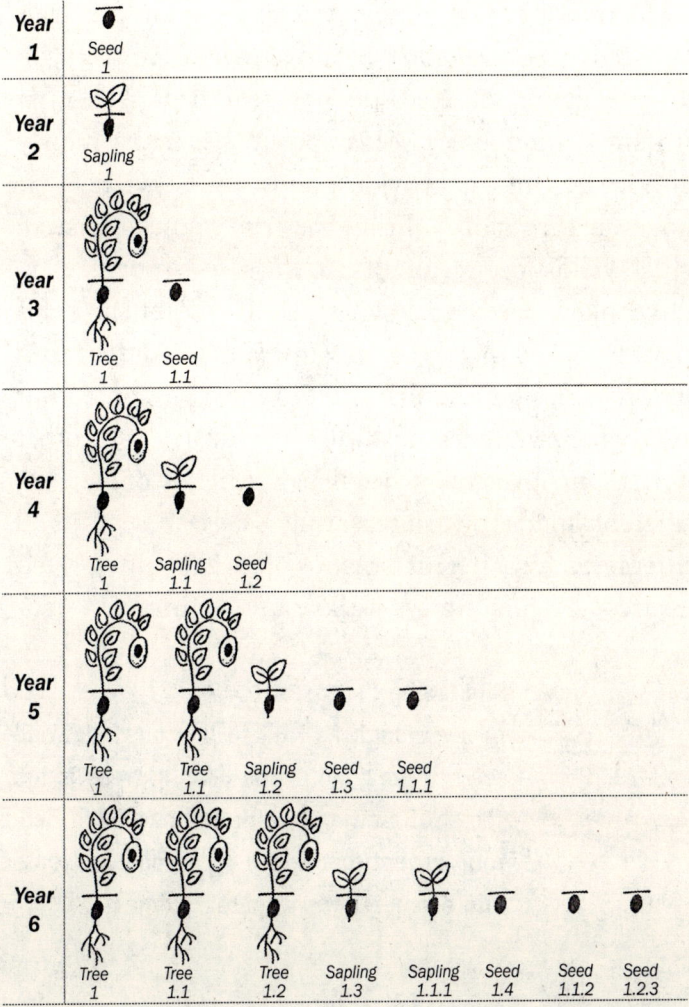

Imagine you have a seed that bears one fruit after 3 years. So the fruit can be enjoyed and its seed planted in soil on the third year. By the sixth year, you have three trees from that one seed. The earlier you plant the seed, greater will be the number of fruits you will enjoy.

The trick of making money is to see money as fruit and seed. Fruit we enjoy. Seed we invest. All seeds do not germinate. All trees do not bear fruit. Yet, even if a small number of seeds sprout, we make money without having to provide goods and services. Our money makes money. From the fruit comes the seed, which yields more fruit.

We plant seeds in low-risk and low-return debt-funds first, and then gradually invest more and more in high-risk and high-return equity funds. We spread our risks when we invest in different industries. In other words, our investment needs to create an orchard of different kinds of fruit-bearing seeds that respond differently to different seasons and calamities. That ensures Lakshmi always walks our way in the future.

Shakambari's lesson
To see wealth as fruit to be consumed and seed to grow more fruit-bearing trees is the secret of growing wealth and becoming rich. Your current money must be used to create future money if you want to become rich.

Conclusion
12 Lessons I Learnt from Vedic and Puranic Stories to Make Sure Lakshmi Always Walks Our Way

1. **Is Wanting to Become Rich Normal?**
   Annapoorna's Lesson on Hunger:
   Wanting to become rich means wanting to enjoy and share a comfortable life. And that is perfectly normal.

2. **How Do We Earn Money?**
   Brahma's Lesson on Earning Money:
   To earn money, we must be sensitive to the hunger of customers and provide them with goods and services they want so they give us our due as part of yagna, or exchange. If we do not think of customer needs and demands, we cannot do yagna.

3. **How Do We Lose Money?**
   Brihaspati's Lesson on Complacency:
   We lose money when there is someone who can give better goods and services to the market than us, when there is no demand for the goods and services we offer, or if we become too lazy to take feedback from the market and improve.

4. **Who Pays Our Bills?**
   Agastya's Lesson on Obligations:
   We have to pay our own bills. Most of our bills are incurred even before we start earning. When other people pay our bills, we are in their debt. Sooner or later, the moneylender will demand return, one way or another.

5. **How Do We Save Money?**
   Satyabhama's Lesson on Saving:
   We save money only when we spend less than 90 per cent of what we earn. We must save first and then spend. Saving means paying our future selves first. As a young person we must provide for our old self, rather than hope that our children or family will take care of us. That is the responsible thing to do.

6. **Why Do We Grab Money?**
   Kubera's Lesson on Extortion and Exploitation:
   We grab money when we find no opportunities for exchange, or we have no trust in exchange, or when our hunger matters more than other people's hunger.

7. **How Do We Manage Money?**
   Ganesha's Lesson on Accounting and Planning:
   Accounting and planning are key activities for managing money. Only accounting without planning stops us from thinking long term. Only planning without accounting prevents successful implementation.

8. **Why Can We Never Avoid Taxes?**
   Shukra's Lesson on Fairness:
   We cannot avoid taxes as long as we share the earth with other people, and as long as we cannot give food away voluntarily to those who cannot feed themselves and others.

9. **How Do We Guard Wealth?**
   Hanuman's Lesson on Insurance and Will:
   When we are alive, we guard wealth by insuring ourselves against predictable and unpredictable risks. When we are dead, we guard our wealth only if we have prepared a clear will when alive.

10. **How Do We Attract Money?**
    Vishnu's Lesson on Repeat Orders and Referrals:
    We attract money when we delight our customer with our goods and services so much that they keep coming back, and they even recommend us to others. This is the opposite of grabbing money by cheating the system, tricking the market and exploiting employees.

11. How Do We Share Money?
Varuna's Lesson on Charity and Investment:

We can share wealth by paying our bills, by repaying our debts, by paying taxes. In most cases we share wealth grudgingly, because we are expected to. Sometimes we share wealth with expectations and conditions attached, hoping to change the world, or be remembered for our good deeds. But true sharing is giving money where the returns are not measurable or guaranteed, to feed the other without concern for the self.

12. How Do We Grow Money?
Shakambari's Lesson on Debt and Equity:

To see wealth as fruit to be consumed and seed to grow more fruit-bearing trees is the secret of growing wealth and becoming rich. Your current money must be used to create future money if you want to become rich.

Map of Becoming Rich

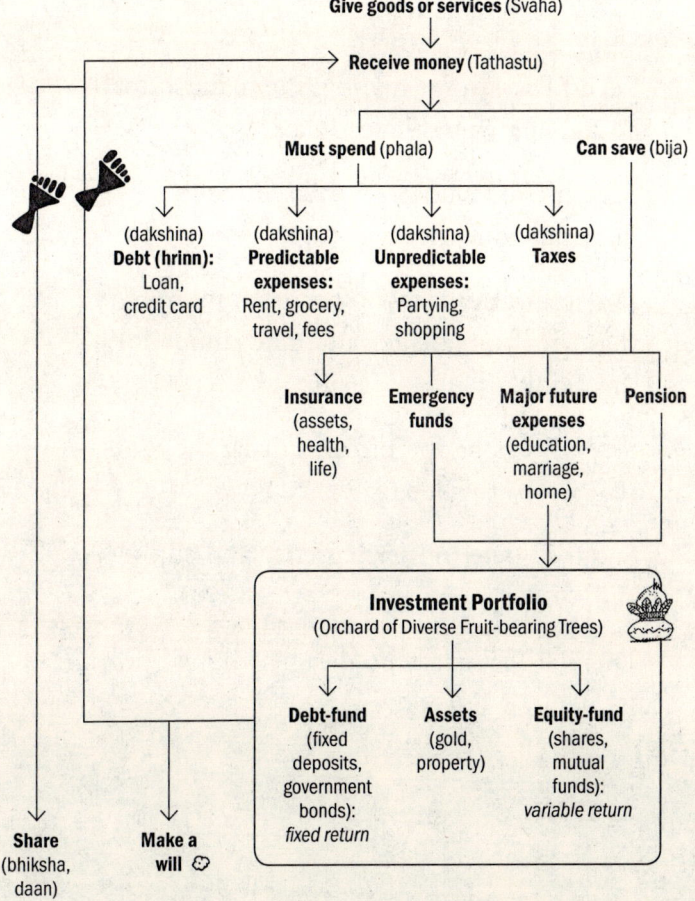

Devdutt Pattanaik

Acknowledgements

Tarun Balram for reading the manuscript and giving valuable feedback.

Suresh Nair who first exposed me to financial education.

Jaideep Ugrankar who has been more friend than wealth manager and a key guide for this book.

Sreejith Chellappan for inspiring thoughts that led to this idea.

Simar Puneet for her patience and editing skills.

Dhaivat Chhaya who designs all my books.

My Gita

By Devdutt Pattanaik

In *My Gita*, acclaimed mythologist Devdutt Pattanaik demystifies the *Bhagavad Gita* for the contemporary reader. His unique approach—thematic rather than verse by verse makes the ancient treatise eminently accessible, combined as it is with his trademark illustrations and simple diagrams.

In a world that seems spellbound by argument over dialogue, vivaad over samvaad, Devdutt highlights how Krishna nudges Arjuna to understand rather than judge his relationships. This becomes relevant today when we are increasingly indulging and isolating the self (self improvement, self actualization, self realization—even selfies!). We forget that we live in an ecosystem of others, where we can nourish each other with food, love and meaning, even when we fight. So let *My Gita* inform *your* Gita.

'[Devdutt Pattanaik's] subjective and diplomatic craft continues to shine through in his new book. [My Gita] marks his transition from mythology to philosophy—one that he makes with deftness and skill.'

—Scroll.in

'While [Devdutt's books are] a quick read, the lessons [they] offer are invaluable and will last a long time.'

—Business Today

[Devdutt] is a master storyteller, often with delightful new nuances.

—India Today

My Hanuman Chalisa
By Devdutt Pattanaik

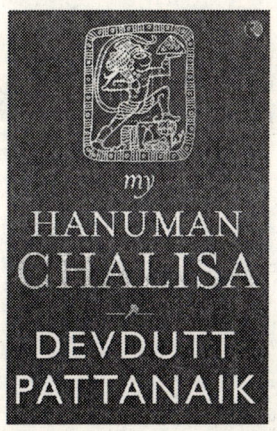

Reflecting on one of Hinduism's most popular prayers for positive energy

Every time we experience negativity in the world and within ourselves, every time we encounter jealousy, rage, and frustration, manifesting as violation and violence, we hear, or read, the Hanuman Chalisa. Composed over four hundred years ago by Tulsidas, its simple words in Awadhi, a dialect of Hindi, and its simple metre, musically and very potently evoke the mythology, history, and mystery of Hanuman, the much-loved Hindu deity, through whom Vedic wisdom reaches the masses. As verse follows verse, our frightened, crumpled mind begins to expand with knowledge and insight, and our faith in humanity, both within and without, is restored.

> 'In *My Hanuman Chalisa,* Pattanaik is at his very best. The book is strewn with his own charming line drawings of Hanuman, as Pattanaik takes each verse of the *Chalisa* and unpacks it, literally, metaphorically and mythologically... Pattanaik uses his considerable imagination and vast resources of information to link the verse and Hanuman to other stories and other ideas across the vast and varied landscape of classical and contemporary Hinduism.'
> —Arshia Sattar in *Outlook*

'Apart from providing simple translation of every verse from Hanuman Chalisa, Pattanaik's book also presents insights into his understanding of these verses and the situations under which they were originally penned.'
—*Indian Express*

'Pattanaik's approach [in *My Hanuman Chalisa*] reveals Hindu mythological figures as concepts that are personified in riddled tales that are easy to remember and entertaining to retell... At the very end, Pattanaik also introduces readers to Tulsidas himself.'
—*Hindustan Times*